PRIORITIZE

FUN FUN FUN

PRIORITIZE FUN

A manifesto for those who want to
enjoy life, not endure it.

NANCI BERGMAN

FIRST EDITION

ISBN-10: 1798237164

ISBN-13: 978-1798237168

Cover image by Mohamed Nohassi, unsplash.com

Cover design by Studio Zilt

www.prioritizefun.com

@prioritizefun

Dedicated to all us over busy, overloaded, and overwhelmed human beings just trying to eke out a little happiness in our lives. Let's wipe the white board clean and consider a new, more enjoyable approach.

TABLE OF CONTENTS

INTRODUCTION..**9**

Who is This Chick and Why Should I Trust Her?

The Beginning

Fast-Forward to Present Day

CHAPTER 1: THE NEW NORMAL NO ONE REALLY WANTED..**17**

A Backstage Pass to a Day in the Life

The Value of Busy

So What's the Punchline?

Enter the Mid-Life Meh

Self-Help to the Rescue

Let's Consult the Polls

CHAPTER 2: PRIORITIZE FUN............................**51**

Time to Get Your Priorities Straight

Contract Negotiation 101

My First No

When in Doubt…Delegate

CHAPTER 3: THE FUN EXPERTS........................68

~~Work~~ Play Like a Dog

Fun Cures All

Fun is Dynamic

CHAPTER 4: FIND YOUR FUN-JO...............….......79

The Two Paths

Some Obvious and Ingenious Ideas

Be Like the Predator

A Backstage Pass to a Day in the Life- Take 2

CHAPTER 5: LIVING THE FUN........................106

Time for Some Serious Debunking

Choose Action

The Fine Art of Procrastination

Regret Really Sucks. No, Seriously

Do or Do Not. There is No Try

CHAPTER 6: SHARING THE FUN......................130

Club Membership

Get Yourself a Sponsor

Avoid the Saboteurs

Prioritize Fun: The Movement

So, In Closing Arguments

INTRODUCTION

Hey there, welcome! I have to assume given the title of this book, you have an interest in the subject matter of fun. Awesome. Me, too. We're sure to be fast friends. But first, some questions.

Do you find it hard to remember the last time you really cut loose, did something daring, silly, or laughed so hard that beer came out your nose? Does all of your time and energy seem to be consumed with to-do lists, chores, responsibilities, and the never ending dramas playing out in news feeds? Do you find yourself looking at your hectic life and wondering why you're not happier? Do you forget what you like to do for fun? Do you even remember that fun is an option? You are definitely not alone.

Prioritize Fun is a simple but very powerful idea. I believe that by having more fun — deliberately, purposefully, and with extreme prejudice — you become happier by default. I think fun is the fundamental catalyst we're missing in our lives that makes happiness seem so elusive. And by actually prioritizing fun as much as you prioritize all of the other important garbage in your life, you'll finally find the happiness you crave. I believe that.

I wrote this book to share my theory of having purposeful fun. It's an exploration of why we do the things we do, how we become trapped in our own lives, and a practical guide on reclaiming our fun-jo. I know us humans have a tendency to overcomplicate things ... myself included. I promise there will be no complex equations, no memorization, no detailed programs to transcribe, no homework, and no pop quizzes. This is not the type of self-help bible that requires a complete personal transformation. Though you may feel transformed from time to time.

No, Prioritize Fun is about getting back to being who you really are. Simple and straightforward.

It's about enjoying your life, not just enduring it.

Who is this chick and why should I trust her?

I'm hoping at this point you're vibing with the concept I'm laying down. But I suspect there may be that little voice in the back of your head thinking ... *wait, who is this person and why am I listening to her?* So I figured a little backstory may be warranted.

There are a ton of "success" markers in life: money, status, friends, job titles, power, physique, cars, you name it. I would say in each of these areas I score maybe a C, sometimes D. I'm still technically "passing," but I wouldn't say I'm the pinnacle of success in any of these traditional measures.

Where I do score an A+? *Fun.* I've been on a constant secret mission my whole life. An aggressive and unapologetic pursuit of fun. No matter what phase of my life I've been in, I've made fun my priority. I wake up every day happy and excited. I'm up for anything and look forward to making the mundane awesome.

(And now you might be thinking, *Something's wrong with her, she needs help.* Or, *I feel sorry for her family.* Or, *She's full of it, no one is like that.* If you think any of the above, I'm glad you're here because you need me).

So how did I become so insufferable?

The Beginning

Conventional wisdom tells us there are two different kinds of people in this world: rule followers and rule breakers. But in reality there's an in-between group. I've been an active rule *bender* since 1975. Never one to rebel to the point of serious consequences, I always had a healthy suspicion of rules that seemed to be overkill and/or interfering with a good time.

"Don't play with matches!" … OK, I get that one, fire is deadly.

"Don't play with the hose!" ... Yeah, no, gotta do it. Water dries, and chasing and squirting your friends is fun as shit.

"Don't run at the pool!" ... OK, I have seen people slide out and get some serious concrete raspberries.

"Don't splash at the pool!" ... Yeah, no, gotta do it. Tormenting my fellow teenage girls and drenching their fresh perms was joyous.

My ability to walk this line of maximizing fun while avoiding trouble solidified my status as "idea boss" in my youth. It came about quite organically. Whether it was building treehouses, choreographing roller skating routines, racing bikes through the creek, or recording fake radio programs on our tape deck, my friends always looked to me to figure out what would be next-level fun.

In college, I graduated from idea boss to party boss. In an environment of limitless possibilities and very limited responsibility (just make grades and don't ask for money) I thrived. You know when you talk to people in their thirties and forties and they recount how their college days were the best time in their life? They had life-altering fun, yet almost feel like they could have pulled their heads out of their asses and embraced the freedom more? Like the saying goes, I wish I knew then what I know now and I would have been crazier. I distinctly remember living my college life with that future realization ever-present. I *did* know then, and I made the absolute most of my time. I was the irreverent sorority girl named "Berg," more focused on the beer slides at Betas than the formal dances or Sunday chapters. I recall sisters telling me I needed to be more serious. But somehow I knew they were wrong. I'd have the rest of my life to be serious. This time was my pass, and I made a lot of hay under that sunshine. I emerged from that haze with an engineering degree and entered the real world.

Like many, I was unsure what my career path would look like. I knew I wanted to be "successful," but wasn't sure exactly what I should be doing. I did know, after sitting behind a computer designing battery pack cases that the engineering life was not for me. This led me to a string of roles at various companies large and small. While I struggled to find my success work-wise, my side business of fun thrived.

I moved to San Diego and created a great new friend group. I found my partner in crime, Rob, who would eventually become my husband. We traveled the world and embarked on new adventures. I maintained my status of party boss, but the parties became slightly more complex. Like city-wide pub crawls and trips to Australia. My friends trusted two-week itineraries to me knowing that, if nothing else, the trip would be fun.

I eventually found my groove in sales. I was a decent salesperson. I mean, I've sold more than my fair share of batteries, headphones, and audio equipment over the years. But if I'm honest, I think my ability to close deals had more to do with my joking demeanor and less about strategic tactics or business prowess. All things being equal with my particular *product du jour* and a competitors' product, buyers would rather give me the order. I was more fun to hang out with. In a sea of endless corpo-speak, boring meetings, and even more boring events, I was often a welcomed change of pace.

Ah, but when I took on my most important role — mom — I gained even more street cred. As a mom to a boy living in southern California, there's no shortage of outdoor adventures, things to jump off of, and general mischievousness we could get up to. And of course we always had a gaggle of little friends in toe. Without really planning it, my parenting style was one that definitely made fun a priority. I was the to go-to choice for kids in the neighborhood for any activity. I was once again idea boss, and since their little minds were new to most things, I appeared to be a creative genius.

Fast-Forward to Present Day

And here we are. Let's talk about the moment that kick-started this deeper exploration of fun and its greater power: My son Dalton was in fourth grade and assigned a hero project. Basically he had to write about someone who was a hero to him and all the reasons why. He picked me, which was already like winning the Super Bowl of motherhood, but it was the reasons he gave in his speech about why he picked me that were definitely unique. All of the other kids in his class who selected a parent listed the usual suspects of attributes: loves me, supports me, is very caring, always helps me, takes care of me when I am sick, etc. My son's opening line was, "What would the point of life be without fun? If no one had the ability to have or create fun we would just chug along with no meaning."

Seriously, he said that. I was in as much disbelief as you probably are. He then explained in great detail how I was the master of fun and, as a result, his hero.

That's when I had my epiphany. I'd spent my whole life trying hard to be good at things. Sales, working out, dressing myself fashionably, engineering, keeping plants alive, home décor, personal finance, starting a business, fixing clogged drains … you name it. I put forth a good effort, but never really kicked ass. Where I really rock, where I consistently kill it, where you can always count on me to knock it out of the park is with fun. It's what I'm uniquely good at.

You know how they always say you should do what you love? It makes sense, of course, but I' never executed on it. All of the different jobs I'd held, companies I'd worked for, projects I tried … when I stopped to think about it, I never really loved any of them. But the idea of inspiring, creating, and sharing fun ... *that* is definitely something that I'm passionate about.

So that's what brings us together on this page today. I fundamentally believe that people have the power to change and shape the lives they want, and I'm an admitted self-help book junkie. Even though I am not a "writer" by any stretch of the imagination, I decided to put pen to paper and to share my theory on fun and its ability to lead us to happiness.

If just one person reads this book and cracks a smile, I'll consider my mission accomplished.

So strap in, let's do this!

CHAPTER 1

THE NEW NORMAL NO ONE REALLY WANTED

We have all had those moments in life when we realize something for the first time. It was there all along of course, but for whatever reason we just never noticed it. Then somehow we suddenly gain a heightened realization to it. As if we awoke to our surroundings. This usually happens to me when I am bested at Scrabble, try to call B.S. on my husband's turn, and as a result learn a new word. Inevitably for the next week I'll hear or see that same word in the wild at least three times. It will be in the article I'm reading. I'll recognize it in a song lyric. I'll notice it on a menu or hear it in a podcast. It's like a magical coincidence from the universe — that mocks me.

Because most people have experienced this in their lives in some way, it has a name; the Baader-Meinhof phenomenon. It occurs when the thing we've just noticed, experienced, or been told about suddenly shows up constantly in our everyday life. It gives us the feeling that seemingly out of nowhere we are surrounded by it. We are not crazy, we are totally seeing it more, but there is a scientific reason our brains process the new information in this way. It is a frequency illusion and our cognitive bias to notice unfamiliar things after they are first brought to our attention.

Recently I found myself immersed in my own Baader-Meinhof situation. Maybe it was because I had a little extra time on my hands. I had just changed roles within my company to one that was more involved with strategy and less with putting out daily fires. This afforded me more hours in the day to actually think about things versus just reacting to the most recent crisis.

Or maybe it was because I couldn't help but contemplate what my next move was going to be in my never-ending pursuit of world domination. During this same time, I'd also made the complicated decision to call it quits on an online business I had been trying to launch and grow by myself on the side — unsuccessfully, of course — for the last two years. Failure always has that unique way of making us reassess ourselves and the world. We can't help but think, *OK, that totally did not pan out how expected, sucks to be me, now what?*

Or maybe, just maybe, it was because I was now officially in my forties and I had a different perspective on things. Having ushered in my fair share of grey hairs I had to assume there was little extra wisdom that came with it.

Whatever the cause, I distinctly remember the moment I paused and really took notice of my peers. I closed the laptop, put down the phone, and quieted all of my inner dialogues and unspoken agendas to really study them. My husband, my friends, my co-workers, my neighbors. Everybody in my bubble of existence. Instead of talking at gatherings, I listened and observed. I took deliberate note of what everyone said and did. And then I noticed it. The singular theme that became overwhelming apparent was they were all so utterly, hopelessly, insanely BUSY.

Even though most of these people had their own unique circumstances and different lifestyles, it was very clear that they all shared this same trait. When I asked any one of them how they were doing or how their week was going, I eerily received the exact same response. "Busy!" coupled with an audible exhale.

Occasionally I would get the added "but good busy!" which presumably would take a little of the stressful edge off. However, this was instantly eradicated by their high pitched tone and clenched, twitching face. It didn't matter who I asked: women, men, parents, non-parents, career people, stay-at-home caretakers, everyone had the same response.

Meanwhile, everywhere I turned, the busyness in action seemed to smack me in the face. People mowing me down on the sidewalk, busy getting someplace super-important. Bagged food rushed to waiting vehicles because people were too busy to sit down in restaurants, let alone go inside and order. Forced conversations with the tops of peoples' heads because they were too busy multi-tasking on their phones to look at me and converse. Once I saw this theme I couldn't escape it. Baader-Meinhof everywhere. Just like that damn 77-point word "chutzpah" my husband Rob pulled out of his ass for the Scrabble win. Now that I was aware of it, the busyness was everywhere I looked in the wild.

As I thought about all of these encounters, I couldn't help but wonder ... these people are busy, clearly, but *busy doing what?*

Of course, there are the usual suspects that add to the busyness in our adult lives like jobs, kids, and general household upkeep, but it's not like these responsibilities have not always existed. Since as long as any of us have been around, people have had to earn money, take care of their families, and provide shelter. Many times under even harsher or more intense conditions than we have today. Yet I firmly believe they did not operate at this current frantic pace. Benjamin Franklin, busy with semi-important stuff like drafting the Declaration of Independence and discovering electricity, still found time to chill out and enjoy his many creative hobbies and leisure time. I can honestly say I don't ever remember my parents or my grandparents ever replying to the question of "how are you doing" with an answer of "busy." Even my first boss many moons ago, who was pretty hardcore, never used the word busy in his daily rantings.

Something had changed.

A Backstage Pass to a Day in the Life

Let me paint a picture, and tell me if this sounds familiar at all.

Butt crack a.m., the alarm goes off with a harsh beep-beep-beep. It jars you from your sweet slumber. For sure this is the same beep that must be sampled in all elevator music in hell. You hit the snooze button a minimum of one, and maximum of three times. It has taken some conditioning over the years, but you come to accept that four times is just egregious.

You roll your stiff body out of bed and hit the shower.

You yell at the kids to wake up. They hit the equivalent of the snooze button on you, but they won't stop at three. You repeat yourself at least four to five times with the threat level increasing exponentially each time to just shy of physical violence.

Now you attempt to make yourself look presentable. Whatever your profession, this involves searching for clothing items on the floor and/or what I affectionately call in my house the "laundry staging area." This is essentially the purgatory of laundry. A space, be it a shelf or allocated corner, that is piled high with clothing. Technically, the clothing is clean, yet in limbo between the dryer and the orderly heaven of your closet and drawers. If you report into an office, then you also need to find a blazer to throw on. It covers all wrinkled sins and instantly makes you look professional-like, or so I like to tell myself. Don't forget to factor in that extra five-to-ten minutes at the laundry staging area as you search for your kid's very specific Beastie Boy T-shirt that must be worn today to prevent a complete mental breakdown.

Dudes, count yourself lucky at this point because once you're dressed you can just run your hands through your hair and let the day begin. No need to even shave, just rock that heavy shadow, you edgy bastard. Ladies, unfortunately you still need to deal with some level of hair and makeup. This is a complex web of actions too intricate to detail here. A gifted surgeon simply cannot explain their craft in layman's terms.

Breakfast time! You hit the kitchen with faint thoughts running through your head about "being healthy." These are quickly silenced as you scan the contents of the fridge and cupboard as well as the time on the clock. First task, get coffee in your mouth. Second task, grab anything in arm's length for yourself and chow.

You then remember that children need to eat to live, so the cereal must be poured and lunches must be made. You give a quick shout out to your man James Caleb Jackson, the inventor of cold breakfast cereal, because without his contributions you might actually be forced to have to cook something. You haphazardly pack lunch knowing that 80 percent of the contents will be either traded or thrown in the trash. Your sole responsibility here is to make sure you don't pack any peanuts, or any nuts in general, dairy, gluten, GMOs, sugar, etc. to avoid the angry reminder from school.

Finally, the last scramble to locate all lost items such as shoes, homework, coats, and bags. In these final frantic moments, you navigate the Matrix of your house with the intensity of Neo searching for a land line.

Commuting time! Whether driving straight to the office, school only, or school then the office, or straight into errands, or maybe even the liquor store, one thing is certain ... there will be traffic, someone will be doing it wrong, and you will be pissed.

Now time to spend your day on a hamster wheel of never-ending action items while dealing with frustrating personalities and cranky individuals ... your coworkers and/or kids.

Commuting time (Part Deux)! - see above.

The day is almost over, time to start your two side businesses of car service driver and tutor. It is imperative that you maintain your five-star rating as an efficient on-time driver so as to not incur the wrath of the various coaches. If you have a carpool arrangement in place for practices, it may seem like you have a leg up, however you need to account for the ten-plus back-and-forth daily texts coordinating details with the other parents.

Once home you must dust off your student hat, relearn math, and provide instruction. Forget any distant memory of addition, subtraction, multiplication, and fractions that may still dwell in the depths of your brain. You are not able to just give the correct answer anymore. Figure out the five different ways to solve the problem to assist your frustrated kid, and oh, don't forget to show your work.

Dinner time! The options are cooking or delivery. You weigh the guilt against the pain and the mess. Either choice presents the same scenario of endless negotiation with the kids on exactly how many vegetables must be consumed for them to be paroled from the table and eligible for dessert.

You can now see the finish line. Clean up (or said more appropriately, putting the dishes in the sink to "soak" for a couple days), bath time, tuck in, and you are done. As in, cooked. Kaput. Forked. Of course these final tasks always take longer than they should, and then you remember that one email that has to go out tonight, and oh yeah, the family pet has some business to discuss.

Done! It's late. You're exhausted and barley able to keep your squinty eyes focused on whatever form of screen you are looking at. The weekend will be here soon, right? If only you can survive until then, right? Right?!

Wash, rinse, repeat for the next day. You tell yourself that at least you're one day closer to the weekend, and the likelihood of survival is increasing. Every hour and day of the week is tracked with the fervency of a Jason Bourne manhunt.

And then Saturday finally hits.

But the sad truth is that even when the weekend arrives, everyone is just as busy as they were during the week. There are commitments of sports, recitals, family gatherings, supply replenishment missions or, even more depressing, work. Employers care less and less about the sanctity of personal weekend downtime. In fact, America is one of the only industrialized nations without any laws restricting the number of hours in a work week. According to the International Labor Organization, this results in Americans working 137 more hours per year than Japanese workers, 260 more than British workers, and a staggering 499 more than the French. That is twenty full extra days we could be dipping our croissants into our expertly made café while enjoying a mime routine to the sound of accordion music. We Americans dedicate more and more of our hours as our workloads pile higher and higher, blurring the lines of the work week and the weekend.

All said and done, we ultimately just end up surviving the weekend as well.

sur.vive- verb- continue to live or exist especially in spite of danger, hardship, or ordeal. *Against all odds he survived several assassination attempts.*

Well, that sounds fucking awful.

When given a choice, who would ever want to just survive life? Particularly when - if you draw the timeline out far enough - literally no one survives it. Don't we all want to *thrive?* It seems like the answer would be an obvious yes, yet I see people making the conscious choice every day to cram pack their lives to the point at which survival is the only real option.

Although the day in the life recount of our hero is fictitious, it is actually nonfiction. I witness those exact same activities with my own eyes occurring every single day around me. It plays out over and over like the hideous monotony of Billy Idol's worst ditty "Mony Mony". Don't get me wrong, I love me some Billy and his snarls are world-class, but the endless repetitive refrain of that song could drive any sane person to madness. So why would we subject ourselves to that?

Why had we all collectively agreed to be so freaking busy?

The Value of Busy

Culturally, today it seems we have latched onto this notion that we have to be busy to be valued. Our busyness basically defines our worth and status. In a *Washington Post* article called "Why Being Busy Makes Us Feel So Good," the author Brigid Schulte claims that people actually compete over being busy. He says, "If you're busy, you're important. You're leading a full and worthy life. Keeping up with the Joneses used to be about money, cars, and homes. Now, if you're not as busy as the Joneses, you'd better get cracking."

We have convinced ourselves that if we aren't doing something every second of every day, then it's essentially a waste of a day. And we're a waste of a person as a result. Having idle time on our hands now equates to not being relevant.

This social shift seems to have its origins in the business world. In a paper published in the *Journal of Consumer Research*, authors Silvia Bellezza, a professor of marketing at Columbia Business School, Neeru Paharia of Georgetown, and Harvard's Anat Keinan (a.k.a. some serious smart people) discuss how a busy and overworked lifestyle, rather than a leisurely lifestyle, has become the new aspirational status symbol. Where traditionally researchers had analyzed how people spent their money on products to establish status, in America this is now shifting to the study of how people consume their time. They draw this conclusion from a series of studies that showed positive responses given in correlation to participant's busyness and lack of free time. The perception is that a busy person possesses desired human capital characteristics like competence and ambition, and therefore is scarce and in demand in the job market. These are the rock stars, the ninjas, the corporate mavericks that all the employers court. The top innovative companies want them, and we all want to be like them. We all desire to be sought after. Who doesn't want to be picked to go to Top Gun, to be the best of the best?

But here's the thing: This mentality has crept into pretty much all of our workplaces, not just the elite corporate scene. Our culture has come to valorize compulsive overwork as the only path to success in any vocation. Reference any media coverage of a successful person and you will quickly notice some common repeated themes. These individuals are praised for their unwavering devotion to work, obsessive drive, shunning of leisure, and their superhuman ability to not require sleep. These laser-focused people are celebrated in their various areas whether they are start-up founders, students, scientific researchers, food truck owners, non-profiters, or even artists. They all subscribe to the hustle and even proudly brandish the word on their coffee mugs, social media feeds, and hoodies.

Now, a solid work ethic is undoubtedly required if we want to achieve our goals, but the lines today get blurred between the hustle and the grind. While the hustler is revered, the grinder is someone that will work tirelessly without the same reward. Their sense of fulfillment is just being part of the chaos, of juggling multiple tasks, and moving at a breakneck pace. We have created this aspirational ideal of working that is rarely achievable, and never sustainable. That is why the only hustle I personally subscribe to is the groovy 70s disco dance.

If I look back at my own experience in the workforce over the years, I can definitely recognize the slow but steady ratcheting up of busyness. When I started out at my first corporate job, if people were able to leave work early it was inferred that they were efficient, focused, and able to get things done. Now the same behavior is perceived very differently. Today, even if someone gets their job done, there is this pressure to fill any and all available hours with more. If they are brazen enough to leave work early, they receive an unspoken (and in some cases definitely spoken) judgment of laziness and apathy about their career.

We seem to want our collective time to be overscheduled and frenzied. Or perhaps we're simply terrified of what might happen if we don't. When I walk into my current office, I see my coworkers racing from meeting to meeting clutching their laptops and half-eaten power bars all day long. When five o'clock rolls around, many haven't been able to come up for air since they came in that morning. It's now considered ridiculous to think you can talk to anyone without scheduling the ten minute conversation in their Outlook calendars. No one has any extra time, and everyone feels good about that.

Is that normal? Should it be?

I remember the days when we all agreed the workaholics were the assholes. The Bill Lumberghs, quintessential upper-management scumbags who are not only obsessed with TPS reports but would continually ruin Peter's weekends by forcing him to not only come in on Saturday, but Sunday as well. But no matter how much we hated our personal Lumberghs at the time, I'd be willing to bet in today's work culture we'd see it play out differently. Peter would be viewed as more of the loser for lounging around in bed instead of working. We would question if he had any purpose or direction. Any worth. Ummm, yeeeah, what is he ahh doing with his life? He better start ahh hustling....mmmkay.

It would be one thing if this desire for busyness was contained to just our careers, and perhaps that would be somewhat manageable, but our personal lives have been methodically getting more and more jam-packed. The fact that people today have to white board their social schedules is definitely a clear indication of this occurrence. I have friends who are booked out several months. The attitude is if we don't have multiple events and parties to attend every weekend, then we must be lame and unimportant. Likewise, if we cannot rattle off at least three personal projects and/or hobbies we are involved with, then we must be dull. Or lazy. Or unworthy. No one wants to be ordinary, boring, and lack sparkle. Everyone is busting ass to get promoted to the VP of Personal Time and Executive Director of Fabulous. Really, anything below Director level just won't cut it anymore.

Alarmingly, the busyness trend isn't isolated to us adults either. We have pushed this agenda onto our kids as well. Humor me for minute while I wax poetic about my simpler, slower placed, provincial childhood.

I had an interest in soccer, so I joined a team and started to play. I was pretty good, not great, but had fun and enjoyed the sport. We had one hour of practice and one game per week. We won some games, we definitely lost some games, but we always had good camaraderie as a team. The season lasted a couple months. I was never going to be a professional soccer player and somehow I and my parents and my coach and everyone else involved in the affair were okay with that.

Fast forward to today, and I now have a son interested in soccer. He joined a team. He is good, not great, but enjoys the sport and has fun. He most likely is never going to be a professional soccer player either, yet he has two 90-minute practices a week and one game. The season lasts year round (a.k.a never ends). Additionally, there is supplemental Futsal training, as well as a series of full-weekend travel tournaments. These tournaments are not just a couple miles down the road from your house either. We're talking hours away in some cases. Soon the out-of-state and even international tournaments will be happening. I would not be surprised if the next team correspondence announced we will be doing several weeks of deep woods soccer training, Rocky-style, to prepare for our upcoming Russian tournament with Ivan Drago's team. Some good ol' log chopping and beard-growing along with dribbling exercises.

With this insane time commitment, I can't help but ask myself ... is this really necessary? Does this one activity of soccer need to make us this busy? Did I enjoy my soccer games any less as a kid without all of this scheduling? I don't think so. And the fact that I have real concerns as a mom about soccer burnout for an eleven-year-old kid is kinda crazy, right?

It *is* crazy. According to a poll from the National Alliance for Youth Sports, about seventy percent of kids in the United States stop playing organized sports by the age of thirteen because "it's just not fun anymore."

That is truly somber. Sports, which was originally designed for leisure and to build teamwork, has been transformed into an unpaid job our kids want to quit after being forced to punch the clock for several grueling years. Talk about sucking the joy out of something, sheesh.

And remember that workaholic mentality where more and more precious hours are being stolen from our free time? Well, our kids are not immune and face the same situation with school and homework. The ten-minute rule which is a standard endorsed by the National Education Association and the National Parent-Teacher Association states that students should do ten minutes of homework per grade starting with first grade. That translates to ten minutes in first grade, twenty minutes in second grade, and so on. In a 2015 *American Journal of Family Therapy* study involving more than a thousand parents of children in kindergarten through grade twelve, researchers found children in the first grade had up to three times the recommended homework load. Even more shocking, they found that kindergarteners, who are not supposed to have any homework, were doing up to twenty-five minutes a night on after-school assignments. Let that sink in folks … twenty-five minutes. Twenty-five minutes of colors, shapes, and letters is pure torture for the five year old and the parent alike. Imagine being strapped to a chair with your eyeballs forced open *A Clockwork Orange*-style and being forced watch the Wiggles perform "Wheels On The Bus" on loop.

Yeah, it is something like that.

Even when it isn't our jobs, our social lives, or our kids, we still manage to cram in some extra busyness in our lives. It's understandable that we all want to feel productive and socially accepted, but in our quest for this we tend to be over zealous. The desire to be busy and valued can overtake sanity. If there happens to be some unplanned time within our schedules, we feel compelled to fill it up, and often times with unnecessary things. Things that add zero value to our lives or goals and do nothing but overstretch us.

Again, this goes back to the fear of being judged and socially downgraded if we don't *want* to do all these extras. We feel compelled to one-up each other on busyness. So we say yes more often than we should. There will always be a school meeting, a friend's 5K run, a neighborhood volunteer group, a brunch, a church fundraiser, you name it. Most times when asked to join, we automatically say yes without even realizing we did so, or fully understanding the commitment. In reality, unless any of these activities hold significant interest or meaning for us personally, we should probably just say no. But that can be tough. As a society we say yes for a variety of reasons, including guilt, but most importantly because it just seems so much easier than saying no. The irony however is that even though it may be more comfortable in the moment to say yes, in the end we become uncomfortable dealing with the added stress — and resentful.

I absolutely hate to bake. A lot of people love to, and thank God, because I do enjoy eating more than my fair share of tasty treats. I most likely hate it because I suck at it, but that stems from the precision and discipline it requires. The rigidness turns me off from the get go. The way I muddle through my culinary exploits is a fly-by-the-seat-of-my-pants method. There shall be no measuring, and there shall be no predetermined cook time. I just throw it all together in a skillet adding the ingredients that I think may taste good, judge when I think it is done, and nine times out of ten it pans out decently. Cooking just has way more flexibility. Even overcooked pasta with vampire-killing levels of garlic is still technically pasta, and hence edible by definition. With baking, that does not fly. Any miscalculation or misstep on preparation and you're screwed.

"So," you ask, "why in the world would you volunteer to bake for a bake sale?" Well, I am not immune to the knee-jerk yes, either. There I was, chatting with some other moms in the schoolyard when the request was lobbed into the group like a grenade. Before the words fully connected with my brain, I blurted out, "Sure, I can do that." Fast forward a couple days, and there I am, pissed that I have to make a special run to the store for the ingredients. There I am grumbling in the kitchen trying to follow the recipe. There I am agitated monitoring the oven, and soon after, there I am seething that I have to systematically cut off all of the burnt parts. There I am not a happy camper, and resentful that I made the commitment in the first place.

In simple terms we often do activities to people-please, and don't have fun doing them. It is no wonder we get bitter. According to research from the University of California, San Francisco, the more trouble you have saying no, the more likely you are to experience frustration and burnout. People-pleasing, like chronic overworking, is just not sustainable over time. Not to mention it's exhausting. We will always reach our breaking point.

Still, even when we don't have others adding to our busyness, we do it to ourselves. We feel we need to fill every second of time, so we unconsciously create meaningless busy work. It is task-driven, yes, but inconsequential in the grand scheme of the day, week, or life. Is it really necessary that we scroll through our entire Instagram feed? Does every cupboard in the kitchen really need to be organized monthly? Will the world end if an email is not answered within ten minutes? Does every detail of everything we do have to be perfect? I'm sure it doesn't, but that doesn't stop us from Patrick Bateman-level obsession over insignificant things like business cards.

So What's the Punchline?

Ok, ok ... so it is evident that we are all busier nowadays, and quite possibly unnecessarily. But who's to say that's all bad? One could argue that our busy, overworked lives will ultimately lead us to our end goal or purpose that much more quickly.

Maybe. But I think that argument depends on what we are chasing.

So I asked myself, *what do most of us really want out of life?*

With a doozy of a question like this, I decided to consult my all-knowing buddy, Google. I typed in "what do people most want in life" and a million links loaded. After reading through top ten lists a-plenty, psychology papers, business journal articles, blogs, and personal quizzes, the indisputable winner was, wait for it, *happiness*. Happiness is what most people want out of their life. *Well, duh*, I thought. Happiness has held top search rankings with us humans for centuries now. It was a mere two thousand seven hundred years ago when the Greek philosopher Aristotle claimed that the purpose of human existence is to achieve happiness. Happiness also happens to be one of the central themes in all of the world's religions. Cool, it's settled. Happiness it is….check, please. Everyone live like SpongeBob and laugh out loud all day without any reason and annoy the miserable people.

Seems straight forward, but not so fast. It is not a one-size-fits-all thing. The problem with happiness is it's hard to define on a universal scale. Happiness means something different for everyone. It is unique to someone just as much as their preference in music or favorite foods might be. Even worse, what may make one person happy may have the opposite effect for someone else. I absolutely love roller coasters, and have my whole life. From my first ride on the Racer at King's Island with my dad, to the Accelerator I rode with my family last summer at Knott's Berry Farms, every experience has been equally exhilarating. I love the adrenalin rush and typically can't remove the smile from my face for an hour after the ride.

My friend Jen on the other hand has a very different relationship with roller coasters. From her first trauma-inducing ride as a kid, to her reluctant vomit-producing ride with her own kids, her experiences have been less than rad. She avoids them like sushi from a gas station.

Although we try to paint in broad strokes with themes like health, wealth, and charity, I think the devil truly is in the details when it comes to happiness because details are what really matter to us as individuals. And when we have a hard time being honest with ourselves and defining what makes us happy, it becomes harder to achieve and even harder to hold on to. Happiness eludes us because we don't always know ourselves that well, nor take the time to figure it out. I think most of us can admit that it's tough to dig deep, and even tougher to be honest with what makes us tick.

So what do we do? Many people just grab onto an ideal of what *should* make us happy on paper. We tend to seek happiness from outside sources, whether it be our job, a spouse, a family, a title, a certain number of digits on a paycheck, or a fancy house and car. This makes happiness an ever-moving target that is most likely missing the real mark. Sure, people and things in our life can bring moments of joy, but because they are elements outside of who we really are at our core, they never deliver meaningful and lasting happiness.

We all want to believe that after Sam stressed so hard over the affection of hot-guy Jake Ryan in his even-hotter red sports car, he gave her complete happiness for the rest of her life. More likely she had some great sex and later in life ended up with a soft-hearted nerd because that's who she is at *her* core … someone a little nerdy and willing to give up her panties to help a geek.

Couple our inability to define with certainty what happiness for ourselves looks like with the barrage of busyness destroying each day, and it's not shocking that that we find ourselves at a bit of a loss.

And then it happens …

Enter the Midlife Meh

Throughout our lives we must battle unique adversaries. Early on our enemies are likely the "school expulsion monster" and the "getting knocked up demon." Later on, we match wits with the "they're just not that into me balrog" and the "fired from job dragon." We are no strangers to the struggle. But midlife brings us a new foe.

The successful tactics we employed in the past to overcome our enemies are ineffective with this new guy. And so he springs on us seemingly out of nowhere ... the "disillusionment sloar". Many of us right now know what it is to roast in the depths of the sloar, I can tell you.

This guy is like all other opponents on steroids. His superpower is his ability to make us question everything in life. *Is this all there is? ... What's the last memorable thing I did? ... Why am I not happier? ... Is life just a series of action items? ... Would my younger self be disappointed in me?*

By the time the disillusionment sloar arrives at our doorstep, we have usually passed most of our major mapped life milestones. We learned to talk and walk, check. Passed our driving test, check. Graduated from school, check. Stayed out of jail except for that one time, check. Became a functioning member of society, well, check-ish. Got married, check. Had a kid, check. Hmmm, what's next on the list? I wonder ... oh yeah, DEATH. Mayday, pump the brakes!

Now, some of you may be thinking that our encounter with the disillusionment sloar has all of the makings of a good old-fashioned midlife crisis. We are all familiar with this phenomenon coined by psychologist Elliot Jaques in 1965. He described the term as a time when adults reckon with their own mortality and their remaining years of productive life. The midlife crisis conjures dramatic images of Lester Burnham smoking pot and hitting on high school girls, Thelma & Louis careening off a cliff, or Frank the Tank streaking through the quad. We even give that knowing look to each other when the neighbors get divorced and acquire new cars, new younger partners, and new surgically-enhanced anatomies.

Outside of these dramatic changes, what I believe happens even more in the wake of the disillusionment sloar isn't the midlife crisis, but the midlife meh. Instead of the epic end-of-movie battle scene with flying fists of fury and explosions that come with a crisis, the midlife meh conjures barely a wisp of drama and can go all but undetected. The term "meh" refers to that which is lacking in interest or enthusiasm. It is both uninspiring and unexceptional in every way. And that's why it's so sneaky and dangerous. A crisis infers a situation that requires and gets immediate action. A hurricane, political unrest, and health epidemics are examples. These are real serious problems, and they garner the focused attention of very smart scientists, world leaders, and doctors dedicated to solving them. The mid-life meh is the complete opposite.

It's not good for sure, but not quite worthy of pressing the panic button. Neither us nor a team of experts are committed to working tirelessly around the clock addressing it. We have the ability to recognize it, but often just limply accept it. We

41

convince ourselves that it's just our new norm. This inaction is exactly why the meh is so threatening, and what gives the disillusionment sloar his advantage and ability to defeat us.

Now even though we may not be prepared to sound the alarms and pull out the heavy artillery reserved for a crisis, we do often seek out guidance while the midlife meh cloud looms over us. If you're anything like me — and I suspect you are, given the fact that you have taken the time to read this awesome book — you look for a plan. Something new. Something different. Something that can make you a little better and possibly clear out the meh. Never one to fully give up, you know there must be someone or something that can help you course-correct a bit. So you put on your fedora like a badass, strap that whip to your belt, and enter that knight's cave to find your holy grail. You are confident in your ability to choose wisely. You are smart enough not to be tricked by any false grails like that Nazi-loving dude who shriveled up like the Crypt Keeper.

Self-Help to the Rescue

There really is no shortage of ways you can improve yourself. You can discover a new purpose, start a new diet (insert trendiest fad here), launch your own business, get involved with a charity or cause, learn to meditate, feng the shui out of your surroundings, read a book every week, exercise (insert trendiest fad here), chase that promotion, embrace mindfulness, make more money, get up early in the morning, study yoga, go back to school, yada, yada, yada, and one more yada for luck.

Admittedly I've always had a bit of a fascination with the self-help genre, eagerly consuming anything related to new business and healthy living strategies. I have at different times in my life attempted three big ones on this list: meditation, strict dieting, and starting my own business. There is no argument that these are all very noble pursuits, but what I found is that these endeavors required me to make a big change in who I was organically. This may seem obvious on the surface, but until you're in the trenches struggling, it is hard to conceptualize. They required me to get super serious and up my level of intensity. I needed to execute on goal-setting, create complex action plans, enter calendar reminders, diligently research, consistently journal, and use a whole lot of extra brain cells … basically a level of commitment rarely witnessed outside of Mrs. Roper's commitment to muumuus. So my dalliances in these pursuits were short-lived.

But why? you ask.

Well …

I'm so not a morning person, so every time I woke up early to start my day off right with meditation, the only measurable result was that I was crankier than usual. Not to mention the fact that I was never successful in "clearing my mind." I don't think my brain came equipped with an off switch. There's simply too much useless pop culture nuggets stuffed in there waiting for a free second to burst free, like the *Alien* from Kane's chest. So meditation and I broke up.

Like everyone, I wanted to detox my body from the decade of debauchery known as my 20s. Plus, being older I was much more aware of the need to be healthy. My newly formed spare tire — at this point a10-speed tire, thankfully, not yet monster truck sized — served as a daily reminder, as well. Enter the juice cleanse with all of its touted benefits. It became very clear that as a natural born carnivore, juice was never going to be a viable substitute for a meal for me. I probably should have considered Fight Milk over the juice. So the diet and I broke up.

For my online business, which we all know how that turned out, I went into an industry I knew nothing about. Not only that, but I sold a product I didn't even use myself … customized 3D-printed jewelry. I got caught up in the business plan, the cool factor, the competitive opportunity, and what it could be based on my financial models. It took exhausting levels of engagement to build the operation from the ground up and then try to maintain it. Levels that were never going to be manageable with just one person. Jewelry was just not in my wheelhouse of things I was excited about, and it was hard to connect organically with consumers. I had always made my statements verbally and not through accessories. So my bruised ego and the website broke up.

If what we pursue is not aligned with who we really are at our core, it's going to be tough to post the win. And let's be real, I think it is difficult for any human to maintain a high level of ferocity on something no matter how well-intended. In fact, former Harvard psychology professor Dan Wegner has asserted that "too much concentration on set goals can lead to the exact opposite of the desired goal." He coined the term "ironic processes" to describe the failure of positive mental processes when performed under conditions of stress.

A good example is sports. The more you obsess over the perfect golf swing or the perfect free throw shot, the more likely you are to choke. Similarly, the more you obsess over every calorie you put in your mouth, the more likely you are to eventually binge on tasty burgers when the meat perfume wafts by you. Thanks, Dan, for making us all feel a little better about our starts, stops, failed attempts, and just plain failures.

But here's the deal folks: Let's say we were successful in adopting these new practices into our lives, ultimately making ourselves better …

… and let's say we're even cool with adding to the complexity of our already self-imposed over-busy lives …

The truth is, there is no guarantee that any one of these actions will lead to our true desired result. And if you recall from before, our collective goal as human beings is to have happiness in our lives.

So why do we do this to ourselves?

We've all heard that doing the same thing over and over and expecting a different result is the definition of insanity. There is truth to this no matter how much we want to pretend it's just an urban legend (or worse, a personal development cliché). Why do we always have this urge to make things more complicated than they need to be? And why, when we demand a guarantee on everything else in our lives from car safety to Sham-Wow purchases, do we digress on a guarantee for happiness?

It seems to me that we could all be approaching this the wrong way. After all the failures and false-starts, I felt that there really had to be a much simpler way to find some sustained happiness. A way that's enjoyable. A way that's more natural and less structured. A way that doesn't perpetuate this endless cycle of intense busyness programs that fall flat. A way that's at least a *little* more foolproof.

Confucius said, "Life is really simple, but we insist on making it complicated." I couldn't agree more. I decided that I was going to invest my time and brain power noodling on this issue and find a way. I was done with conventional thinking. I was also fundamentally opposed to anyone settling for meh. That's just too sad. Like a sundae without sprinkles. Who wants to stare at bare whipped cream? I sure don't. If our existing realities are serving us bald sundaes, I was ready to fight back and deliver a gnarly throat punch. Over the next week I treated this issue like a crisis. I dedicated focus and tireless hours. I questioned everything.

And then it hit me with a stunning strike of clarity: FUN.

Fun is the problem. And the solution. Nobody's having any pure fun anymore. And if they are, it clearly isn't enough. We have all become a bunch of Dean Wormers. We have kicked the Delta brothers out permanently and burned their house to the ground. No more fun of any kind.

Fun is the missing link.

Let's Consult the Polls

To validate my theory, I decided to run a poll among my busy peers. It made sense given it was their observed actions that kicked off this journey for me in the first place. The question was simple: "What was the last thing you did for fun for yourself?"

I then had a follow up question: "How long ago was that?"

I wanted to determine if my friends/neighbors/co-workers were ever having fun, and if so, at what frequency. I made sure that I did this research face-to-face, interview style. I needed to ensure the responses were spontaneous and not rehearsed or pondered for days as they stared at an email. I've always been told that a person's first reaction best represents what they really think, so I wanted to capture that, as well as read their body language.

I set off and started asking my questions casually by the mailbox, on soccer game sidelines, during school pickups, and at the coffee machine at work. All said and done I reached out to about fifty people in my circle. The first thing I noticed was people's facial reaction to the questions themselves. It was a scrunched up, raised brow, and overall confused look. Almost as if I had asked Bill and Ted to explain the financial crash of 2008. It did not seem to compute. Sometimes I was just met with a blank stare. It was clear to me they were not getting asked this question on a normal basis, nor thinking about fun regularly. When they did muster an answer, the responses ranged from a little lame, to disconnected from them, to suspiciously manufactured.

Some examples of what I would classify as lame were "cleaned out the garage" or "escaped the family for an hour at Target." Granted, I am judging based on my own bias, but I think we can all agree that neither of these activities would jump to the top of any traditional fun list.

In terms of disconnected responses, many cited activities designed around others' fun. Mainly, their kids. This is all well and good, and they are obviously caring parents, yet it seemed like the events were very one-sided and hence did not address the original question of what THEY did for fun for THEMSELVES. There are a million fun ways to hang with your kids and do something you both enjoy, but I would argue that binge watching *Peppa Pig* or dads escorting their daughters to the nail salon don't really qualify as mutual.

Frequently I questioned the validity of answers. The responses felt disingenuous, like what they should say versus what they really wanted to say. I could almost feel their fear of judgment as they considered their response. It made me recall the first time I put together my resume. Like everyone, I didn't have a ton of experience other than graduating school, so I needed to add in fillers like hobbies. But when I thought about what my real hobbies were at the time, I was pretty sure that I shouldn't list drinking, hanging with my friends, and lying out at the beach. I was conditioned to know that I needed to say *something* that sounded better. Something with a greater purpose to make me appear better and more well-rounded. So gardening and volunteering it was! Yup, that is what a lot of answers felt like. Fake hobbies, not real truths.

When it came to the response of "how long ago was that?" things got really fuzzy and vague. It was hard for most people to pinpoint when they were having their fun if it wasn't an established event like a holiday, birthday, or vacation. I repeatedly got the impression that the fun they said they had was infrequent and in the past.

Oh, I was definitely on to something. Fun did seem to be missing from everyone's daily lives, and hence could really be the missing link.

CHAPTER 2
PRIORITIZE FUN

So is the secret to happiness as simple as just having more fun? Yes, I think so. The way I see it, happiness is the result we are seeking, and fun is the catalyst. A catalyst is that which precipitates an event, or in other words the action needed to achieve your desired result. Without the proper catalyst, experiments are doomed to failure. We all learned early on in our classrooms that the foamy baking soda lava will not erupt out of the paper mache volcano without the vinegar catalyst.

Based on what I experienced in my lifetime so far, I'm just not convinced that any drastic transformational self-improvement regimen or a jam-packed schedule of activities are real catalysts for happiness. I see people engaging in these activities all of the time, and I also see those same people not exhibiting much joy. Right at this moment, there are millions of people around the world that are toiling at the gym, cramming for an exam, working late in at the office in hopes of a promotion, or force-eating kale for dinner (the nasty raw kind, not the kind smothered in delicious bacon bits), and guess what? Not a smile in sight. To me this means, at least some of the time, that the busyness/struggle catalyst is failing miserably in the happy experiment.

I also don't believe that you can just force yourself to "be happy" if you are not. That feels unnatural, and not really doable outside of a 45-minute faking it period during the office Christmas party. You can't just sit there and will your brain to happy without actually doing anything to facilitate it. The Dalai Lama said it best: "Happiness is not something readymade. It comes from your own actions." So it seems the sheer-will catalyst is also failing the happy experiment.

What I do know with 100 percent certainty is that I have never seen anyone having fun that wasn't happy as a result. Whether it is a group of bros playing pickup basketball, a couple enjoying a concert, a family watching a funny movie, grandmas playing bridge, girlfriends joking over a glass of wine, or even just a little girl jumping her way to triple digits on her pogo stick… when people are engaged in fun, the smiles and happiness are inevitable. It is just a universal truth. Like the fact that pizza and beer is the world's most perfect marriage, or the fact that Han shot first.

Now, you may say, *Isn't having fun and being happy the most obvious observation in history, ever?* And I'd say, *Yeah, but if it's so friggin' obvious why are people so chronically miserable?* You can't say something is obvious if the majority of people can't or won't engage in it. It is often the obvious and simple things that we most lose touch with in life.

In fact Margaret Heffernan, author of *Willful Blindness: Why We Ignore the Obvious at Our Peril,* explores in great detail the human condition in which we choose, often unconsciously, to remain unseeing in situations. We should technically know something, yet don't because it makes us feel better not to know. This mechanism of keeping ourselves in the dark grows out of all the small daily decisions we make that anchor us in affirming beliefs and values. We start to see less and less, while at the same time feel more comfort in the familiarity with greater certainty. We think we see more even though our personal landscapes shrink. She proves this phenomenon through case studies ranging from failing marriages to business reform to preventable health conditions.

Considering this in the context of happy, you can see how deciding daily to be over-busy affirms that *busy* is the only valued catalyst hence limiting our ability to see any other alternatives.

So sure, being happy as a result of having fun is not revolutionary, but I believe it is a notion that most of us have become blind to. It is no longer in the landscape of our lives or what we feel familiar with. Being carefree and surrendering to fun helps you connect again with who you really are at your core...and relishing in that. It's letting go of the need to over-structure and curate everything, and bathing in the beautiful chaos of what is. It's becoming familiar with yourself again.

For my family and I, skiing has always been our tried-and-true fun activity. No matter the mountain, or weather conditions, every time we are flying down the hill together a-hootin' and a-hollerin' we are fully immersed in the fun. We start when the lifts open and don't stop playing until they close. And on a warm spring day, we never pass up a "suns out guns out" opportunity on the slopes. I cannot recall a single ski vacation where we're not all at the height of our happy game. Even when our toes are frozen, we get lost on the trails, or have a gnarly wipe out...we are persistently basking in the thrill of it all.

The same definitely can't be said for some of the other trips we have embarked on together. There have been the wedding/graduation/birthday weekend jaunts. The obligatory family related travel. The over-scheduled, different city every night "vacations". And while there have been moments during these excursions that were worthwhile, none can compare to the fun-first ski adventures.

The bottom line is you are guaranteed to be happy while you're having fun. Like, money back guaranteed.

If we look to science, the guarantee becomes even more apparent. Amit Sood, MD, professor of medicine at the Mayo Clinic College of Medicine, spent two decades reading thousands of research materials, meeting with hundreds of scientists, and studying tens of thousands of patients to understand how our minds interpret thoughts. He concluded that the human brain is continually switching between two modes: *default mode*, when our minds are distracted and/or wandering, and *focused mode*, when our minds are engaged with something interesting.

Sood's research shows that our brains are in default mode for at least half of our waking hours, and that's when we're vulnerable to thoughts that can bring us down. While it's necessary to be in default mode to help us make connections, be creative, and brainstorm, Sood believes we spend too much time there. We're more likely to obsess over what-if scenarios or spend too much time thinking about what people "really" think about us. Thoughts kick in like, *I wonder if Jerry is mad at me? He hasn't been returning my emails lately. He is most likely pissed since I took over the Underhill account. Damn, I promised myself I was going to be more of a team player at work.* This causes stress, depression, anxiety, and a general lack of happiness. And he's right. Think about your own default mode.

Conversely, when the brain is in focused mode, we tend to feel happier because we are taking in something that interests us and we have fewer distractions. We're in the moment. Sood cites focused mode for allowing us to fully engage with the world, and to appreciate its novelty and meaning. When we participate in activities that are uniquely fun for us, and by definition are things we have extreme interest in, it makes sense that our brains switch to focused mode and as a result we feel the happies.

I think we can all agree computer geeks Gary and Wyatt were fully in focused mode when they invented the bold idea to turn a Barbie doll into a living sexbot. And arguably there is no one more vivacious or fun inducing than Lisa.

So yeah, good news ... it really is that simple.

Time to Get Our Priorities Straight

Too often people incorrectly think that fun just happens and weaves effortlessly through the hours of our day. It doesn't. You have to pursue fun and make it happen. Fun requires action ... our action. And the number one way to consistently act on something is to have it top of mind.

Prioritize it.

The good news is the vast majority of us definitely know how to prioritize, as we are forced to do it every day juggling our jobs, spouses, and kids. Some of us prioritize and don't even consciously realize we're doing it as we face hundreds of little daily decisions. Priorities serve as our life Sherpas to point us in the right direction. Every action we take and every decision we make will either put us that much closer or that much farther away from our goals. Whatever it is that we have established in our minds as our own personal priorities is ultimately where we give our focus, time, and attention. We as humans act based on what we deem is important to us.

The best evidence of this phenomenon I've ever seen came when I was dating. It didn't matter if I was in an early relationship with a stressed-out corporate guy, or an out-of-work artist/surfer. If they were into me, I became a priority to them. No matter what they had going on in their lives, they would always magically find and make the time to be with me and give me focused attention.

Conversely, if they were not really that into me and/or on the fence, I would not be a priority to them. And with that would inevitably come the never-ending list of excuses: crazy roommate drama, family visiting, work travel, dog sitting, deathly ill … you name it. The bottom line is they would only make time to hang out with me when nothing better was going on. Harsh but true. We are all guilty of this though, myself included. Priorities are powerful. Even Gandhi will back me up on this one, as he famously said, "Action expresses priorities."

So just imagine for a moment if we all made fun a priority. What if getting enjoyment out of each day was neck-and-neck in ranking with clearing our inboxes? What if fun wasn't considered a luxury unattainable in everyday life? What is we didn't treat fun like a reward, only allowing ourselves small amounts of it here and there, but only after powering through the drudgery and the *busyness*?

Now I'm not suggesting we completely abandon all responsibilities and use this theory as an excuse to throw on a pair of pajama pants, pour a Caucasian ala The Dude, and embark on a life of total leisure. We all have important things that warrant our concentrated attention, like keeping ourselves and our families alive. But if happiness is truly our life's goal, then we need to find some balance and make it — and, by default, fun — a priority.

So what's the holdup? Guilt, for starters.

We harbor guilt when we do something just for fun, just for ourselves. It seems selfish. We feel guilty when others aren't having fun, or can't have fun. We feel guilty when our fun could be perceived as inappropriate. Selflessness is revered in our society, not selfishness. Ask someone how their Saturday was and it's hard for them to admit, "You know, I took a couple hours to go for a long walk with my dog and play. Then I vegged on the couch with the kids and watched classic Yosemite Sam cartoons. And oh my God, I got a bellyache laughing as he beat the horse/camel/dragon mercilessly on the head. I almost forgot that when he says whoa he means *whoa*. It was really fun."

Doesn't that description feel wrong somehow? Lazy? Selfish? I mean, that description includes taking time for our own enjoyment instead of having an actual deliverable to show for it. But more than likely that time spent having fun was just what the happiness doctor ordered to help us recover from our hectic week of stress and agitation. We need those moments of enjoyment to regain our sanity and maintain us on our track for happiness.

Know what? We should feel okay to own that. After all, as adults we're the ones in charge of our lives. We don't have anyone else to take care of us. So if we aren't a little selfish and put our needs and goals first from time to time, we are making a mistake. We should not aspire to be selfless, we should aspire for balance.

There was a time when I would feel a pang of guilt because I wanted to enjoy my coffee on Saturday and Sunday mornings and read my trashy magazines before pouring myself into the day's events. It was only a small sliver of time, but I couldn't help but feel like I should be doing something more productive like cleaning up the living room or making everyone pancakes. Scouring through those magazines looking at the glossy pictures and captions is mindless, but it's my fun little escape. Sometimes you just have to know who wore it better, dammit! One day I decided to be a little selfish, let go of the stupid guilt, and just enjoy my forty five minutes curled up on the couch. That's when I realized how foolish I'd been. What was I thinking? Ultimately being happier in the morning, and more caffeinated, made for better balance and better breakfasts for all anyway.

Looking at it from a different side, there are real, serious consequences when we don't allow ourselves to have fun. As Marc Bekoff, Ph.D, cited in *Psychology Today*: "Recreational deprivation has been linked to criminality, obesity, and declining creativity." He chronicled the work of Stuart Brown that studied the childhood play histories of male criminals. He catalogued more than six thousand people over the course of his career and Brown writes "What all these studies repeatedly revealed was that normal play behavior was virtually absent throughout the lives of highly violent, antisocial men, regardless of demography."

Serious scary stuff. So it would seem that Jack Torrance's threatening repetition of, "all work and no play makes Jack a dull boy" in *The Shining* was spot-on. Are all us joyless folks destined to freeze to death after chasing our kid with an axe? Of course not. But we can be left angry, bitter, and full of dark feelings if we allow joylessness to dominate our lives and the lives of everyone around us. There are true long-term ramifications to denying ourselves fun and play.

I see fun as a basic human necessity no different than food. When our bodies are hungry, they give us a signal in the form of a hunger pain. We know what to do, and act immediately to feed ourselves and resolve the issue. We prioritize. For some, it's a priority above all else. My friend Steve basically can't function when he's hangry, so we all oblige his snacking no matter what we're doing. Seems like common sense, right?

I wonder why, then, when our bodies give us the signal that we're down or stressed or blue, do we not act immediately by having some fun to remedy it?

That's the big question. Let's figure out how to answer it.

Contract Negotiation 101

So how do we go about changing our priorities? Since a priority is basically a contract we make with ourselves, why not consider the process a contract negotiation? We have been cast to star in the blockbuster movie called *Our Life*. Most of us don't have Arie Gold in our corner ensuring we get the biggest salary, a producer credit, and a primo trailer on set. We are going to need to roll up our sleeves and negotiate our contract for ourselves. For our own fun. For our own happiness. After all, don't we all want our lives to score at least 95% on Rotten Tomatoes?

Like with any contract negotiation, there is going to be some push and pull. Some clauses will have to be stricken in order for better, stronger clauses to be added. We can't just say, "Add fun!" and not make any other adjustments. We can't miraculously create twenty-five hours in a day (trust me, I've tried). Some activities in our lives may feel in conflict with the fun we are trying to add. So how do we attack this? As the renowned conflict-resolver Bruce Lee says, "It is not a daily increase, but a daily decrease. Hack away at the inessentials."

Inessentials. Yeah. When I think about inessentials I can't help but consider our modern digital overload. The 24/7 onslaught of texts, snaps, emails, and social posts create an environment where urgency trumps importance. There are so many ways now in which someone can ping us for their "urgent communication," which nine times out of ten would not be classified as urgent or even mildly alarming. Walk around any public area and you can't help but notice chiming watches, buzzing pant pockets, and of course people bumping into you with their phones blocking their faces. We have become Pavlov's proverbial dogs. The second we hear that ping, no matter what we may be doing in that moment, we have the same response...stop and avert attention to that device (salivation levels vary).

We are trapped in the what's happening right now cycle instead of the bigger picture. A lot of research has emerged touting the need for digital detox, but when we quantify our digital compulsion in terms of time the results are staggering. *Time* published a special edition magazine called The New Mindfulness in 2018. In the article, "Do You Need Digital Detox?" statistics were given on exactly how much time the average person spends on a smartphone.

47 = average number of times per day people check their phones

30 = average number of days per year women spend playing games on their phone

11= the number of accumulated years a person will look at their phone over a lifetime

That last one is painful. Over a decade of lost time. How amazing would it be to reclaim some of that time for fun? Even just a little portion would have a huge impact, right? Of course, the answer is yes, but that doesn't mean I don't sense the collective eye roll. I get that it may be unreasonable to completely unplug in our world today, but I know from my own life that it's possible to cut back. Simple adjustments really make a difference.

Because I am a simple creature, the out of sight/out of mind philosophy worked for me. During non-business and weekend hours, my laptop stays closed and my phone stays tucked away in my bag. I check it once in the morning, once midday, and once in the evening. Removing the distraction from being ever-present allowed me to let go of the temptation to be constantly connected digitally, and let me be more connected in the moment to what I was doing.

I will admit that when I first started ditching my device it seemed weird, almost like I was cheating on it. The anxiety of *omigod what if I need to check something* creeped in. I just reminded myself that I was able to function and navigate this world like a rational human when I was eighteen years old and my best device option was a Walkman. Somehow I always met up with my friends. Somehow I was able to locate the restaurant I was looking for. Somehow I was able to purchase the things I needed. That simple mind fuck and a trail of breadcrumbs did the trick.

Tech is an easy target, but there are plenty of other inessentials lurking around most of our lives. To identify these, it can be helpful to get an outside perspective. Without Polly, would Reuben have come to the harsh realization that he was spending 8 minutes a day, 56 minutes a week, and an astonishing 2 days a year transferring decorative throw pillows on and off his bed? She helped liberate him from a task he was mindlessly considering essential. Sometimes it is a friend's simple *why are you doing that* question that opens our eyes to the needless time wasters.

My First No

Another inessential to hack out: Time suck projects or events we're not invested in. We discussed earlier our nasty habit of saying yes to things we don't really want to do as a social cop out. We find it hard to let other individuals down and lack the courage to say what we really mean. This habit is worthless because it actually benefits no one. *Well, what about the other person*, you ask. No dice. We get overstretched and resentful, while the receiver of our time gets our crap attitude and half-assed effort.

Simple: We have to be better guardians of our time and brain bandwidth. To be better guardians, when asked for our involvement in something we should start with the "no" in mind. We can then let ourselves be convinced to say "yes," but by then we've had a moment to really consider how much skin we want in that game. If no is no, just say, "Thanks so much for thinking of me, but I can't."

Don't forget this next part: Leave it at that. No further explanation needed.

Our impulse to provide a reason/excuse/explanation gets us in trouble and can lead to drumming up lies, which is never good.

Even though I should have learned my lesson from that damn bake sale fiasco, delivering my first "no" felt uncomfortable and it was *definitely* hard to hold back on offering an excuse. This time the activity was crafting, which is also a nemesis of mine. Like baking, the reason for the hatred of crafting is probably the fact that I suck at it. I can't cut materials in perfectly straight lines and write in glorious calligraphy all while not burning myself with a hot glue gun. The required attention to detail is just too much. So when faced with the invite to craft some fall succulent decorations, I knew in my heart of hearts the answer must be no. Like ripping off a band aid, I did it. "Thanks for the invite but I can't" echoed in my brain after I said it, but I managed to offer a friendly grin before I slunk away to my car.

In the end it worked out better for everyone. My friends didn't care I wasn't there, they were just trying to be inclusive. I was happy to spend my time doing something I preferred and enjoyed. And clearly the succulents were happy to not be tortured by me. The takeaway is that it's OK to people-please to some degree. You just need to edit the list of people you're trying to please and make sure *you* are at the top.

I have now successfully executed double digit "no's" and I ain't looking back. I promise, after you deliver your first no you'll find they only get easier and easier to do … just like tequila shots!

When in Doubt…Delegate

Finally, if we take a hard look at what we're responsible for on a daily basis, I am pretty positive tasks exist that need to be done by us, the whole us, and nothing but the us. But many do not. Delegation is a beautiful thing. It allows us to remove inessential duties so that we can give more attention to the things that matter most to us.

Delegation comes easy for some. For others, it's much tougher. If you are a Monica Geller-level control freak (positively Gellerian, as they should say, but don't), delegation is a foreign concept. But if we can release our death grip of control over everything, even just a little bit, I'm sure the world would continue on.

Ask: Are the tasks we control controlling us? Are they genuinely contributing to our life goals? If not, and they can be delegated, delegate the shit out of them! Is it imperative that the bed be made each morning by you? If it adds to your own personal happiness, then cool, do it. If it is a pain, and you'd rather spend that time in the morning having donuts with your cat then delegate it to your bedmate, or if you sleep solo, cut it all together. Confession time. I haven't made my bed in the morning since high school graduation day. Removing that dreaded task from my life has been legendarily awesome.

Now that we've amended our life contracts, cut out some inessentials and bad habits, and made room for fun to be a priority, it's time to start having some. But what is the best way?

CHAPTER 3

THE FUN EXPERTS

Whenever I get introduced to new ideas or concepts, I always like to research the pros. Those who seem to understand or execute it best. So I asked myself, *Who is the Joe Montana of fun?*

But because fun is so personal, and different for all individuals, I found myself — mistakenly — wracking my brain for the one person who'd be a good relatable example to all.

The more I pondered this, the more I began to see that it is the "how" of fun, not the "who" of fun, I was seeking. It doesn't really matter who the person is, or what particular activity they enjoy. It's about how that person is able to prioritize and realize their own fun that matters. I was interested in the execution of fun. How we can release all of our hang ups and just surrender to the experience? How do we not worry about how we look? Or what other people's opinions will be? How do we have a dedicated focus on the fun itself? It then became very clear which experts I was searching for …

Kids and animals.

Kids? They come into the world prioritizing fun before they even know what a priority is. They see something and think, *wouldn't it be cool if I smashed/built/created/hit/played with that?* Then they do something amazing. Without thought our consideration they just do it. This is usually followed by a squeal of delight and laughter, which is literal joy bursting from their body.

For kids, everything is exciting and new. Heck, even solid food offers some giggles. A baby thinks to himself, *Hmm, what is this mushy stuff, feels weird, maybe I should fling it against the wall. Even funner I'll fling it on mom's face!* and one second later the mashed peas are soaring.

Music is another discovered excitement. Search YouTube for "kids dancing" and you'll see endless videos of children unapologetically swinging to the music with horrific dance moves. They couldn't care less what anyone thinks They're into the funky rhythm and they're gonna show it.

Skipping, riding a bike, hitting the baseball, or jumping into pool for the first time. Absolutely exhilarating for kids. Even just playing outside is an adventure. It's about that unbridled excitement of being set free. The rousing thrill of unknown possibilities. Kids identify something fun they want to do and just execute. They aren't encumbered by overthinking, or worried about scheduling. They seize opportunities and make them enjoyable naturally. Adults? We don't surprise and delight in things anymore. It reminds me of the classic quote by George Bernard Shaw, "We don't stop playing because we grow old; we grow old because we stop playing."

The definition of play is to exercise or employ oneself in diversion, amusement, or recreation. You play for the righteous hell of it. Because it is fun. There are no other ulterior motives.

Even as kids start to assimilate responsibility in elementary school, they still do a kick-ass job prioritizing fun. Even though we adults like to use the phrase "work hard, play hard" few actually do it (and those who say they do still make it an endurance test by putting in long work days followed by long nights getting shitfaced, er, *playing hard!*). It truly is our kids who deliver on this slogan. They may buckle down and do some spelling for a while, but rest assured when that bell rings, it's on!

The existence of recess itself is proof that we as a society understand the importance of play. Ask a teacher if kids are better or worse students when they get no physical outlet during the day. Well, yeah…duh. The American Academy of Pediatrics backs this up. They recommend recess as a necessary break in a child's day to help optimize a child's social, emotional, physical, and cognitive development. Their magic number: 60 minutes of moderate to vigorous activity or play daily, as well as sufficient breaks, to help kids mentally decompress. Makes total sense.

So who arbitrarily decided that this shouldn't apply to adults as well? Imagine if we could just get back to our roots of playing as kids, and have recess at work. I really don't believe our basic needs as humans change with age as much as we think. We still need that feeling of release and fun.

~~Work~~ Play Like a Dog

One of the major perks of living in San Diego is access to the beaches. My absolute favorite beach is a little stretch of sand called Dog Beach. This is a designated area where no leashes are required and canines can run free. I don't own a dog myself, but I still love to go there and watch them play. It's such a pure representation of fun and exuberance. Although the humans are undoubtedly enjoying themselves at the beach, these critters seriously take it up a notch.

Animals are pro-level players. They'll play with each other, humans, or even eagerly with their own tail if alone. You don't ever see them holding back on their instinct to frolic and romp (except at nap time). Ever see a dog running free in the grass, jumping with glee, rolling around? If the word joy could be captured in a single image, that would be it.

For dogs, especially, it's all play or waiting to play. They just crave interaction and leap with anticipation for not only their owners to get home, but what's to come on their walks outside. Roaming around the neighborhood, sniffing and exploring everything, all while saying hi to every passerby.

And let's not forget our feline friends. As a nation we are obsessed with uploading, watching, and sharing cat images and videos. I myself am guilty of this and a total sucker for a cute kitten trapped in a cardboard box. It's tough to get an accurate count, but it is believed the daily number of uploads is between 2 to 4 million. Why are they so popular? Cats are inherently fun-loving and inquisitive (when they aren't plotting the downfall of their human keepers). They climb, have unbelievable balance, and perform insane acrobatic moves. Watching them play is simply irresistible to human viewers, and hence the viral nature of the content. We can't help but crave that playfulness.

It makes sense that domesticated animals indulge in fun and play, as they don't have much on their plates in terms of responsibility outside of destroying the couch. We owners take care of all of their basic needs. But play is also very common in the wild.

If you have ever seen a group of otters, it is instantly obvious that these guys know how to have a good time. Their well-known antics include sliding, juggling pebbles with their paws, wrestling, and even playing tag. Seeing them engage with each other puts a guaranteed smile on anyone's face. And don't even get me started on garbage pandas. Their level of mischievous fun is off the charts. Romping around in the night with their black masks, a group of raccoons could steal a bucket of KFC from Fort Knox all while giggling infectiously.

But it is not just the cute little mammals that get in on the fun, their more fierce and dominant brothers and sister subscribe as well.

In a story by renowned biologist, naturalist, and author Douglas Chadwick called "A Quick Bear Story," he writes, "While science can't quite bring itself to say that grizzlies like to goof, the experts acknowledge that, young or old, these bears do devote an intriguing amount of time to play behavior. Exuberance is part of what defines them. So is a strongly developed sense of curiosity".

Even within the complex dynamic of grey wolf packs, fun is on the agenda. The omega wolf, who is the least respected pack member, often serves as the class clown, prodding the other wolves to play in order to relieve stress.

When you think of the intense pressure that wild animals have in their lives, constantly on the hunt for food and evading predators for survival, it is remarkable that play is still integral to their existence. If they can find the time to have fun for their overall wellbeing, then for sure we humans sitting at the top of the food chain with our fully stocked refrigerators should be able to squeeze some in.

The takeaway here? For me, the common theme with kids and animals is that they don't overthink it. They do what feels good in the moment, what makes them happy, and they just go for it. Grown-up humans? Not so much. And we're worse off for it.

Fun Cures All

If we really stop to think about it, fun is not just the answer, it is the super cure for whatever may be ailing or broken in our lives. All those roadblocks in our relationships, jobs, or attitudes that pop up on our path to happiness. Introducing fun can smash through them all.

How can I strengthen my marriage? When you think back to when you first met, all of your time was spent getting to know and enjoy each other. You didn't have any obligation to that person outside of having fun together. You would go on entertaining dates, try new restaurants or experiences together, and plan cool getaways. You would hit up the Fucking Catalina Wine Mixer together every year. Reintroducing those moments of carefree fun back into your married life will remind you why you wanted to spend every moment with that person back then, and ultimately make you want to spend every current moment with them now. Jim never gets tired of playing pranks with Pam. It is their shared love of high jinks that brought them together in the first place, and has kept their bond strong through the years. Rediscover your own Dwight as a couple, and have some fun with it.

How do I be a better parent? There are a million books on the specific do's and don'ts to rearing children. I remember the initial pressure I felt as a new mom to be educated on everything. But the simple answer is to just have fun with your kids. Play games together. Get down on the carpet and roll around. Be silly and obnoxious. More than anything, kids crave their parents' attention, and when you are engaged in fun together, they're getting it. They will forever remember the fun times you played together far more than how tidy you kept their rooms or how many perfect meals you made. Whenever I play the "Remember When" game with Dalton, it is always our silly moments that he fondly recalls above all else.

How do I build deeper relationships with my friends? We have people that we are friendly with and people who are truly friends. The difference is often the level we know and understand that individual. In most social interactions, people have their guard up. They're worried about being polite or judged. But when you engage in fun together, people let loose, drop their facades, and give you a glimpse at who they really are. Great friendships are born in moments of laughter. Bevis never loved Butthead more than when they were in the middle of an epic crank calling session. And those friendships only strengthen when new experiences are shared. Lenny and

Squiggy were already a solid buddy duo. But when they unleased Lenny and the Squigatones on the world, their relationship truly harmonized.

How can my work be more rewarding? We all get a sense of accomplishment when we are able to achieve desired goals at work, but that doesn't always mean we feel fulfilled. Especially if all the goals are isolated and individual targets. I have had way more fist pumping moments throughout my career when I was able to get a complex project across the finish line with the help of a team. These may not have been the most important projects to the company's bottom line, but they were still meaningful and fun to work out creatively. When we get more involved with our coworkers and team members, have fun together, build camaraderie, and attack challenges together, the wins ultimately have more meaning and the losses are less painful.

How can I be more productive? When faced with a task or project, if you have a little fun while doing it, it's amazing how quickly you'll be able to complete it. Our procrastination naturally kicks in when we need to do something but don't want to. Adding the fun part makes us more apt to want to do it. As a result we actually execute, and the quality of results rises in step. Have to buy a card for teacher appreciation day? Yawn. Just another thing to add to your errand list. Maybe you will get to it in a couple days. Instead, how about organizing some students to decorate said teacher's car Just Married-style to show appreciation? Now that sounds way more fun and enjoyable to execute.

How can I get more enjoyment out of each day? This is an obvious one, but do more of the things you enjoy each day. Give yourself those breaks, those moments of fun, and those intriguing adventures you keep putting off. Target some smiles, and you will find yourself smiling more often.

These are just a small sample of the questions we ask ourselves all the time about bettering our lives. And the more questions you ask, the more you will discover that fun is the answer to them all. I know I have.

Fun is Dynamic

Fun is never static. When we dedicate ourselves to fun, it will ebb and flow through our lives in different ways. It'll grow, shrink, twist, change, and in the best cases, squirm beyond our control. What you think is fun at one point in your life may be very different at another. The fun you have in January sledding, building snowmen, and guzzling hot chocolate will be different than the fun you have in July swimming, flying kites, and chugging lemonade. The fun you have with your kid when they are five will most likely be different when they are thirteen. What was fun for you at twenty will be *slightly* different at forty (that's sarcasm, but only a little). Sure, there are nostalgic things from your past you'll always love and enjoy, but there'll be new yet-to-be-discovered things you are sure to love.

That's what is so awesome about fun. It's unique to you, but also has the capacity to adjust, develop, and modify as you grow as a human. Be open to change your concept of fun as you change. As long as you're focusing on the idea of having fun, no matter what shape it may take that day, you'll experience happiness. Remember that no one is judging or critiquing your technique.

If you're smiling, you're doing it right.

"Do anything, but let it produce joy." — Walt Whitman

CHAPTER 4

FIND YOUR FUN-JO

OK, hopefully at this point you're feeling ready to dive in. Happiness is in your sights. You're committed to have some fun and prioritize it. You've cut out some inessentials, and now have some breathing room to do it. You're going to take some cues from our furry friends and lead with your instincts. Ready, set, go......crickets.

The good news is that fun is highly individual. One size never fits all. We don't have to force our personalities or preferences to match some predetermined blueprint of action. And while it is cool that with fun we can basically do anything we want, therein sometimes lies the dilemma. Do what exactly? It's that darn paradox of choice rearing its ugly head again. That gift of limitless choices that unfortunately can lead us to analysis paralysis. So what do we do? How do we find our fun-jo (fun mojo)?

The Two Paths

The way I see it, we have two paths to take on our way to destination Fun Town.

#1 Discover new, exotic, never tried before adventures and embrace the novelty or ...

#2 Unlock the beautiful magic in the ordinary. Do what you normally do, just have more fun doing it.

To execute #1, you need to determine what new adventures make you itch enough to scratch. The world is chock full of experiences from jumping out of planes, to cooking exotic foods, to traveling to new destinations, to learning to play the drums.

I kick this process off for myself by *dreamstorming*, a combination of dreaming and brainstorming. Grab a piece of paper, give yourself 15-or-so minutes, and write down all of the things you haven't tried or done, but want to. This should be free flowing, stream of consciousness stuff. Don't overthink it, and most importantly, remove all limits. Nothing is too crazy, silly, or impossible (or expensive, cuz you just never know!). You don't need to figure out *why* you think something is fun. Go with your glorious, underappreciated gut. You know, your own personal Kuato that you too often ignore to the detriment of both yourself and Mars.

In his book *Blink: The Power of Thinking Without Thinking,* Malcolm Gladwell states, "Our world requires that decisions be sourced and footnoted, and if we say how we feel, we must also be prepared to elaborate on why we feel that way. We need to respect the fact that it is possible to know without knowing why we know and accept that — sometimes — we're better off that way."

Amen Malcolm! There should be no editing on feasibility at this point. Again, we're just trying to expose your initial gut instincts with this exercise. You should feel true excitement for the ideas that you write down. Don't write something just because it's what you think you should want to do (seeing a Broadway show just because everyone else has, doesn't mean you really want to). For me, musicals are my kryptonite. It's important that all ideas be 100 percent authentically you. Have the bravery of Dr. Egon Spengler and just admit that you want to collect spores, mold, and fungus if that's what trips your trigger.

When I did my own dreamstorming, I came up with the following:

1.   Bike roundtrip from my house to the beach
2.   Show my son, Dalton, five countries in Europe
3.   Go indoor skydiving
4.   Participate in a water balloon fight on a massive scale

5. Tackle a double black-diamond ski run with moguls & powder

6. Play the Caddyshack prank and launch a Baby Ruth into an unsuspecting pool

7. Brew my own delicious beer

8. Try to get up on water skis

9. Learn to play pickle ball

10. Go canyoning

11. See NYC during the holidays

12. Catch a fish by myself

Next, you'll want to categorize your ideas by time. This is a critical step to help formulate just how you can integrate them in your life, and ensure they won't end up living like unplayed-with toys in Andy's attic on this piece of paper forever. Place them into short-term, long-term, and special-term categories.

I chose the following qualifiers:

Short-Term = This summer*

Long-Term = Within this year & before I'm 50

Special Term = While in Colorado visiting my parents

*Seasons and weather may play a role depending where you live. Work with it!

Finally, when you think about the activity, decide if it is something you would do by yourself or with someone else. It's never too early to plant the seeds with friends and family to join you on your new adventures.

In essence this is a bucket list, just without the threat of death tied to it. We are having fun here, not contemplating our mortality, so I like to refer to this list as the FUN FILE. It may be tempting to turn this into a project with white boards, spreadsheets, and detailed to-do lists. Avoid that. This is supposed to be carefree, not laborious. The outcome of this exercise is just to land on some concepts that are fun for you. Think "Cocktails & Dreams" in pink neon. We'll figure out the how — and whether we need to jet set bartend in Jamaica to make it happen — later.

So my FUN FILE looked something like this:

This summer I will ….

1.   Bike roundtrip from my house to the beach

2.   Participate in a water balloon fight on a massive scale

3.   Play the Caddyshack prank and launch a Baby Ruth into an unsuspecting pool

4.   Try to get up on water skis

Within this year or before I'm 50 I will …

1.   Show my son, Dalton, five countries in Europe

2. Go indoor skydiving

3. Brew my own delicious beer

4. Go canyoning

5. See NYC during the holidays

While in Colorado visiting my parents I will ....

1. Tackle double black diamond ski run with moguls & powder

2. Learn to play pickle ball

3. Catch a fish by myself

Once you complete a FUN FILE, a cool thing happens. You now have lots of different things to look forward to. Trust me, don't underestimate the power of having something on the horizon that you're excited about. Healthy anticipation is key in energizing our lives. It provides bigger-picture positivity to get us through tough times. Trapped on a conference call from hell? Delayed at the airport? Or worse, waiting in line at the DMV? Give yourself a mental pick me up and pull out your well-stocked FUN FILE. Play with it. Marvel at it. It's *you*. Just imagining your new adventures inspires good vibes and reassures you that your current moment of boredom, bitterness, or existential pain is temporary.

The best part: As you cross things off your list you'll want to do more dreamstorming to keep your FUN FILE full. I've found that the more new things I tried and completed, the more open I was during my next dreamstorming session to things I'd never considered before. You can almost feel your fun-jo rising from the swamp of your previous existence.

Being a working mom, I have always been pressed to cobble together activities and camps to fill my son's summer months. Some were cool, but too many were not really that exciting, had weird hours, and were expensive. With my dreamstorming picking up momentum, I am now contemplating in earnest organizing my own summer camp. It would include our neighbors and friends, be tailored to the activities of real interest to our kids, and keep them engaged during our working hours. Pooling our funds, we would be able to create a predictable budget for hired help. And most gratifying? I would have an absolute blast reminiscing on my own favorite summer experiences while putting together the camp program. Why not? Remember, nothing is too crazy, silly, or impossible for your own FUN FILE.

Executing #2 — injecting fun into everyday activities — in some ways is easier, and in others ways more challenging. We get so stuck in our ways and our daily routines that it's hard to see the diamonds in the rough, as if we have to wake up our brains to the small joys we've been foregoing. Something as small as singing in your car during your morning commute can be as fun as an extravagant party. In fact, as people get older, they tend to find ordinary treats just as joy-inducing as extraordinary ones, according to a study by Dartmouth and University of Pennsylvania researchers. They speculate that older folks recognize the fleetingness of time and are more in touch with it moment-to-moment.

I love to vandalize a good cliché, so let's strive not to just think outside the box about the possibilities of fun all around us, let's take the box, magic-marker the shit out of it, duct-tape wings and two skateboards underneath and ride that sucker down the steepest hill in town.

Getting back in touch with your younger self and what you used to enjoy every day is great inspiration. As mentioned, kids do have the fun gig on lock. So take that long leisurely stroll down memory lane. Crack open those old photo albums, get in touch with childhood friends, and challenge your folks to recall your greatest adolescent hits.

Some Obvious and Ingenious Ideas

To help invigorate this awakening, I have put together some ordinary treats you may have forgotten about since you've been adulting all these years. There may even be some here you've never considered. Rest assured that I've personally test-driven all of them, so I can vouch for them being awe-inspiring … *if you just give in and let them be.*

Ride a Bike. Sounds simple, right? But when was the last time you rode a bike? It is amazing ... truly. There is something about peddling in the outdoors with the breeze tickling your cheeks. I personally love my bike more than most of my possessions. I think it stems from my childhood because my bike was my first taste of freedom. As long as I was back by dinner, I was allowed to peddle wherever my heart desired and explore. I get that same sense of freedom even now when I take off. So drag that sucker out of the garage or go rent one. Have a nice solitary ride, or involve the whole crew. Whatever you choose, embrace the freedom and find some new places to explore.

Strut to Your Own Theme Song. Who could ever forget the famous opening scene of *Saturday Night Fever* with the Bee Gees blaring and Tony strutting down the street in his skintight pants? He *owned* the street. If the music wasn't so loud you'd all but hear the collective whisper of the crowd ... *who is this cool dude?* Strive to feel that same way every time you step out of your own front door. All you need is your own personal theme song. There is no predetermined music type or genre, and there is no pressure to adopt "Eye of the Tiger" ... although, hey, that is a solid choice. The song you pick just needs to speak to *you.* Get you jazzed. Make you feel like a confident badass. My song is "Get Funky" by Teenage Fanclub. Somewhat obscure, this prize ditty has great guitar riffs, well-timed hand claps, and a general build up that lends itself well to leg kicks at the end. Short and sweet it does the job. Every time I play this in my mind, whether I am walking into a crowed bar, strolling the aisles of Rite Aid, maneuvering through the office, or cruising into our neighborhood pool, I can't help but smile and know I'm badass.

Eat Dessert Whenever. Remember when dinner was basically the 20 minutes of previews you had to sit through to get to the main feature ... dessert? Why have we all but given up on this magical part of our daily feasting? Oh, we binge on sweets, for sure. But it's a soulless endeavor. And now that we're older we're aware of calories, pancreas abuse, and the fact that sugar can be evil. But there are times where an epic sit-down dessert experience is just needed and will bring joy and delight. I say go for it. Don't always deny yourself. I guarantee you will have more fun building your sundae bar than you will building your salad bar.

Greet Everyone. If you're like me, you were taught to always say hello, please, and thank you. These are the basic foundations of politeness (and some would say decent society). Lately it seems even if people still mutter these phrases, there isn't much feeling behind it. Greetings are the basic function of communication as humans that allow us to trigger positive conversations. A good greeting connects us on a personal level. A warm, genuine, sincere greeting can cause even a stranger to open up. What's more, greeting someone can bring some levity and brightness to both your days. I can't tell you how many times I've been surprised by a fun interaction with someone new because I decided to greet them instead of putting my head down and walking past them in a hurry. Of course, I like to make my greetings a little more colorful with humor and cheesy catch phrases (Hey there, it's a prett-ay, prett-ay, prett-ay, pretty good day today, eh?). But the choice is yours.

Take a Bath. Taken alone or jointly, you will want to fill the tub with excessive amounts of bubbles and toys. This is not a spa-centric relaxing soak complete with candles and Kenny G (not that there's anything wrong with that). Nor is this the nightly chore of removing the filth layer from the kiddos. The goal here is fun. Splash around and make some puddles. I remember spending many hours when I was young playing with my *Love Boat*-themed Weeble Wobble set. I loved to launch torpedoes at just the right angle to sink the vessel. Rightfully return bathing to a fun experience. The only thing adult about the occasion should be the beverages.

Climb a Tree. There's just something about climbing a tree. Grabbing onto those thick limbs and hoisting yourself up to a high perch camouflaged by leaves. You feel a real sense of accomplishment once you reach this new vantage point. Trees are still (mostly) all around us, yet for some reason we no longer view them as structures to conquer. Big mistake. Next tree you see — weight-to-limb ratios considered, of course — climb that puppy. Then the serious fun can begin as you freak out the people below with a well-timed *Kakaaw*!

Play Kickball or Dodgeball. The reason these sports are so great is that they require very little athletic competency and next-to-no equipment or set-up. This is the perfect recipe for impromptu pick-up games that anyone can play. If you have a rubber ball and some space, you're good to go. In kickball, you get all of the delight of running bases and scoring sans the pressure of whiffing. And I think it goes without saying that hurling a ball at someone in dodgeball is next level gratifying. Who can forget the look of pure joy on Billy Madison's face during his first grade recess session — you know you want to experience that for yourself. So if you find yourself with an extra hour of light before dinner, grab the family and play a quick game in the street. Looking for a change of pace for Wednesday lunch hour at the office? Grab some coworkers for a pick-up game in the parking lot.

Pitch a Tent. Everyone loves a fort. Whether it is a makeshift version cobbled together with blankets and couch cushions or an outdoor rustic iteration crafted from logs and mud, the delight is about being in your own cozy space with your best buds. Tents just make forts super easy. You don't need to plan a camping trip far away in the woods and pack up a ton of gear. Instead pitch the tent right in your living room or backyard. It's the ultimate fort you can pack full of goodies, hang out in, and even watch scary movies or football. It's amazing how a couple of thin nylon walls can transport you to fun town.

Invent Silly Games. A while back my husband and I loved to watch *Three Sheets*, an international travelogue/pub-crawl television series hosted by comedian Zane Lamprey. He'd visit different countries and give the history of their drinking culture while making the rounds to the local spots. He always played this funny game where if someone burped, everyone had to make this hand-to-head gesture. Picture a sideways shaka with your thumb placed against your forehead. Whoever did it last in the group would be the loser, and have to drink. We adopted that game, and have been dedicated to playing it for well over a decade now. My son and his friends all do it as well. There's no point really, but it never fails to be fun and make people laugh. Likewise, we always enjoy playing an abridged version of "Thumb Master" at restaurants while we wait for our food. The point is that silly little games are easy and fun way to connect. Invent your own games, or dig up a classic from your past to play.

Wrestle/Tickle Wars. I remember the feeling of gasping for air as my sides felt as though they would literally burst open with laughter. My dad had a knack for creeping up on me, pouncing, and then locking me in a wrestling hold while he tickled mercilessly. I claimed to hate it, but of course secretly loved it. There's no better physical expression of fun then wrestling/tickle wars. Perfect with your kids, pets, and even better with your spouse. Let loose and attack!

Choreographed Dance Routines. Footloose, Pulp Fiction, Dirty Dancing, and *Rocky Horror Picture Show.* What do all of these great movies have in common? Epic dance scenes. Whether at home or in public, nothing beats busting out a routine with your posse to some thumpin' rhythms. I had a couple choreographed routines in rotation in my twenties and always had a blast performing them with my girlfriends on the dance floor to the shock and (mostly) delight of club strangers. It's some serious fun, and not just for the ladies. Dust off your dancing shoes and throw some synchronized moves together. Lifts and stunts are encouraged as well as any and all incorporations, interpretations, and incantations of The Robot.

Prank 'Em if they Can't Take a Joke. Not exclusive to April Fools' Day, pranks should be enjoyed year round. One of the best things about our kids: They're inexperienced, which makes them perfect marks. There are countless simple and evil little pranks to play on your children. Fake spiders, food switcharoos, a well-timed air horn blast, party poppers attached to bedroom doors, and of course, the classic tape-over-the-remote-sensor. The priceless looks on their little faces once they realize they've been duped is trumped only by your giddy anticipation of the next set-up. I have spent a lot of time crouched behind a bush giggling and waiting to strike. It was time well spent to feed my soul. And I can't wait for the first time they do it to me.

Embrace Wheels. Seriously, why walk when you can roll? That was my motto as a pre-teen when I practically lived in my roller skates. I eventually graduated to rollerblades at some point, but sadly stopped using this as my preferred mode of transport the closer I approached thirty. Having recently attended a party at an old school roller rink, my passion for skates has been reignited. It is a blast to roll along. Whether you are planning an afternoon stroll along the boardwalk/sidewalk, running errands, or simply heading over to a friend's house, consider wheels. Roller skate, scooter, skateboard….pick your preferred poison. That famous saying how it's the journey and not the destination? It'll come to life.

Jump off Shit. I remember one of the first jumps my son took in Catalina Island. He was apprehensive at first, but worked up his courage and leaped into the ocean from a rocky bluff. He hit the water, came up for air, and shouted, "Man, I feel so alive!" No truer words have been spoken. He's now a jump addict, as am I. It can be from your couch, a fence, or a 35-foot cliff into the ocean. Whatever the launch pad, there's no stopping the surge of adrenalin you get from taking that leap. Seize whatever opportunity presents itself and jump.

Shopping Carts. I've had a lifelong love affair with shopping carts. From my first ride as a tot, to careening through the grocery store with my friends as an adolescent, to rolling down the street on a bar crawl in my twenties ... these steel beauties are serious fun. Even now I like to grip the handle like it's a Harley and, of course, make revving noises. I practice my race driving skills as I take corners at high speeds and attempt to avoid the potato chip display. All I can say is, don't knock it until you try it.

Costumes for no Reason. Why should the fun of dressing up in costumes be reserved for just one day out of the year on Halloween (or Comic-Con)? Call me crazy, but I love a good costume, and I love to pepper in some festive pieces into the wardrobe rotation. It can be as subtle as a mole or mustache. Maybe a wig, or a pair of wolf ears, or a jaunty cape. I used to rock my Wonder Women bracelets all of the time when I was younger. They looked super cool, always got attention, and were ready for action in case I needed to fight injustice. Just because we are older does not mean we need to give up the fun. Instead of blindly conforming to the current uncomfortable jean trend, get creative and let the cosplay begin.

Watch the Sun Set. Fiery sunsets have become somewhat synonymous with romance. While dates are rad, we should not stop enjoying them just because we may not be on one. It is like a free art exhibit in the sky. Find a cool spot and take in the majesty. Play some tunes, grab a pizza, share some booze, and enjoy the moment. It is fun to even just pull the lawn chairs into the yard or on your stoop old-school style.

Death Cup. Now we're living on the edge. Now some stakes are involved. Enter Death Cup ... a small-but-potent cup filled with five condiment ingredients of your opponent's choosing. The only rule is that the ingredients must be edible and harvested from the fridge. A classic concoction consists of lemon juice, hot sauce, chocolate syrup, mayo, and Worcestershire sauce. It's not life threatening, as I have personally been the victim of a Death Cup and have survived to tell the tale. It is, however, quite nasty and something you will do whatever it takes to thwart. Death Cup is regularly involved in our mini-golf outings, ping-pong games, and dart matches where the loser has to chug. Trust me when I say it elevates everyone's game, and if I'm honest, is quite fun to watch when you're not on the receiving end.

Singing Telegrams. I love singing telegrams. The surprise, the costumes, the spectacle, and yeah, the singing all add up to some serious fun. It may be one of the biggest tragedies of my life that I have never personally received one, but that doesn't stop me from delivering the joy to others with this lost art. The singing telegram works for so many of life's situations and should be more of the go-to option for reaching out. Maybe someone you know is feeling ill … a headache, fever, and a chill? Ferris Bueller's nurse is the perfect choice to restore anyone's pluck. Maybe you want to celebrate someone's happy event like an engagement, birthday, or promotion. Why send a boring text with stupid emojis when you can delight them with a personalized show choreographed and performed by you? Or maybe your friend or mate is in need of a wind up. Don't underestimate the mischievous fun of a fitting fuck-you gram. Fun for you, fun for the recipient. Everyone wins.

Tag. Anytime's a good time for tag. All you need is the ability to reach out and touch someone with an enthusiastic "you're it" and then muster a little giddyup in your getaway. It is an oldie, but definitely a goodie, with so many possible variations. Who can forget freeze tag, shadow tag, and my personal favorite TV tag? There is no age limit on this game. In fact there was a 2018 film based on a *Wall Street Journal* story about a group of grown men who spend one month a year playing tag. Their dedication and enthusiasm for the game was over the top, and the sole purpose was for insane, extended fun. I love this story and challenge myself as well as you to find some new tag partners.

Nature's Ball Pits. Remember those ball pits at your favorite kid haunt? The thrill you had running and jumping into those million plastic balls and flailing around? If you think about it, leaves and snow offer up the same jump-and-flail opportunity, but without all of the germs and boogers. If you're not taking advantage of this and, as the season permits, building up huge piles to run and jump in you are really missing out. Crunch around with reckless abandon and I dare you not to smile. Hear that? *Dare* you. So get building.

Wear Your Whistle Proud. Maybe it is a Midwest thing, but growing up I always heard the phrase, "Get a whistle around your neck and you think you're God." I have to imagine this pertained to potentially overzealous coaches and referees, or possibly even lifeguards. Well, I'm here to tell you that I've had a whistle around my neck and I have indeed felt like God. There's just something about placing that silver beauty in your mouth and pelting out an authoritative tweet. Equal parts fun and satisfaction. I typically wear my whistle during pub crawls, on excursions with my son and his friends, at the craps tables in Vegas, or anywhere dancing is involved. Really through, I feel like a whistle is an accessory that can be worked into almost any situation (except commercial flights, criminal trials, and maybe — maybe — religious ceremonies). If you're a whistle virgin, order one immediately on Amazon. It is a purchase you will never regret. Even later, in prison.

Leave Secret Notes. Every day during grade school when I opened up my lunch box, I found a special note my mom had written on my napkin. I loved them and always looked forward to them. Along the same line, I leave funny post-it notes for my friends and family in unsuspecting locations. Little inside jokes tucked into shoes, desk drawers, suitcases, pillows, and bags of potato chips. When discovered by the intended victim, they never fail to give them a chuckle and brighten their day. As fun as it is to receive one, I find even more fun to make and hide them.

Friday Night Dance Party. We have a tradition at our house called Friday Night Dance Party. At the conclusion of the week, we push the furniture to the sides of the living room, dim the lights, and crank the music. It is an opportunity to dance like no one is watching and bust every ridiculous move you've got. We often add to those moves by jumping off the furniture with leg kicks (see "Jump Off Shit"). We alternate DJ duties so everyone gets to pick their favorite songs. We started this when my son was fairly young, so there was a lot of Weird Al in the rotation, which made it all the more awesome. If I am honest I still regularly listen to Weird Al. He's a national treasure.

Be Like the Predator

This is undoubtedly just a teeny tiny sample of the different ways in which we can incorporate fun into our daily lives. You may want to borrow some of these ideas or come up with completely different ones for yourself and your family. I like to put myself in the mindset of the Predator. He glides through the jungle undetected while analyzing his full surroundings with the help of his thermal heat mask. When the Predator zeroes in on something like glistening bicep clutching a machine gun, the red and orange colors glow bright, clicking alien noises sound, and critical data feeds scroll on his internal mask screen.

That's how I see the world. That's me, without the mask.

Be like the Predator.

As you walk through your house, office, or neighborhood, assess everything through the view of your own thermal mask. Move your gaze from area to area, object to object, and gauge their potential for fun. When passing a park, your mask may zero in on some swings … they will glow red and you will hear the alien clicking noise. This is your indication to take five minutes and enjoy a swing. Kick up your feet, pump your legs to gain height, feel the wind in your face. Don't forget to jump off for the dismount, and once you stick the landing extend your arms upward like a gymnast for bonus points.

Don't feel like you can only wear your mask during your down time either. "Some 80 percent of your life is spent working. You want to have fun at home; why shouldn't you have fun at work?" asks Sir Richard Branson, aka businessman extraordinaire. Amen, Rich…couldn't agree more! The next time you walk by your friend's desk at work, your mask should zero in on their open garbage pail. Don't pass up the opportunity to shoot a free throw with that crumbled memo you weren't going to read anyway. On a lame business trip? If you're not jumping on the hotel beds, you're doing it wrong. Let your mask guide you, and live out the bouncing dream your mom always tried to squelch when you were a kid. Your nightly rate is the price of admission to this personal bounce castle. If your hotel happens to have a pool ... giddyup and blast out those cannon balls.

Seem farfetched that mentally viewing the world through a Predator mask will make finding hidden gems of fun the norm? Not really. In the early days of the space program, NASA scientists designed an experiment that would determine the physiological and psychological effects of the disorientation astronauts would experience being in the weightless environment of space. They needed to ensure there wouldn't be any negative consequences that could endanger the astronauts or the mission. So they outfitted the team with convex goggles that flipped everything in their field of vision upside down. The astronauts had to wear these goggles 24/7, even while sleeping. Initially they experienced physical symptoms of elevated stress and blood pressure as well as confusion. But between day 26 and 30, all of the participants began to see the world right-side up, even though they were still wearing their goggles. They had adapted to their new realities. They actually created neural pathways that *rewired* their brains to see their world as normal again. This experiment spurred the commonly accepted idea that it takes 30 days for the human brain to create new neural connections that allow it to change a habit and/or its perceived reality.

So in less than a month of diligent mask wearing, everywhere you look will be rife with red glows. You will have effectively *rewired* your brain to see the fun in the ordinary. The unexpected delights hidden in your normal routines. It is the little things that often make the biggest impact.

We should think of our hours, days, and weeks as a long, extended episode of *Scooby Doo*. Sure, the plot was always a variation on the same thing, but the minor tweaks in each episode kept us watching and enjoying. Who's going to be the guilty "Mr. Jenkins" this time? Will the gang decide to visit a haunted hotel or abandoned amusement park? Apply the equivalent little creative tweaks in all the facets of your life so you can keep enjoying it. And of course make sure to keep your Predator thermal mask charged.

As a side note, wouldn't a Scoobie-Doo/Predator episode rock?

Backstage Pass to a Day in the Life- Take 2

Now that we have flexed our fun-jo muscle a bit, let's revisit our hero/heroine (you) and see how your day might play out differently ....

Still butt crack a.m. The alarm goes off but this time the sweet wail of Axel springs you from your slumber. The song of the day kicks in.

Skip the snooze button and roll out of bed. People need to be welcomed to the jungle and they need to be welcomed now.

Hit the shower. As you lather your luscious self, hone your karaoke skills. Remember, it's not the voice but the pageantry that matters. A perfectly placed hair flip and hip thrust makes all the difference. You do remember that no one is watching, right? The question is whether you still care.

Announce the song of the day to the kiddos, and let them know it is time to get up. If they're foolish enough to resist G'n'R, have Alexa blast the real deal in their rooms and throughout the house…that will do the trick.

Initiate the laundry scramble. Rules are simple. First person to dig up all articles of clothing and become fully dressed wins. The winner gets to pick what is for breakfast that day. Oh, and if you report into an office, make sure you throw on a blazer. It covers all wrinkled sins and instantly makes you look professional-like (so I've read somewhere). Chicks get a handicap for hair and makeup, of course (how many minutes will be determined based upon aforementioned complexity).

Breakfast time! Hit the kitchen and let the scramble winner scan the fridge and cupboard. Once they choose breakfast, deal it out to the whole crew. If it happens to be yogurt with a side of Cheetos, just go with it. As long as you get coffee and the kids get a gummy vitamin, all shall pan out. Any unfavorable choices will just put a fire in your collective bellies and up your determination to win the scramble tomorrow. You can sneak in some late night-training if you like after the kids are asleep to assure your breakfast pick. Consider it an adult power-up.

Time to figure out the lunch situation. To strike a balance between ensuring healthy food consumption and not overworking yourself, pepper in a little excitement with the official lunch spinner. This spinner is essentially the spinner harvested from the old *Chutes and Ladders* game that you gave a face lift. There are two possible outcomes: you pack or they buy. Have your kids spin to dictate the outcome for the day. Depending on how you draw the split, and much like Sex Panther cologne, 60 percent of the time it works *every* time — day off from packing lunch! The beauty is the decision was left to fate and your kid's spinning ability. No guilt on your shoulders.

Commuting time! Whether driving straight to the office, school only, or school then office, take your mind off traffic/frustration to have some fun and observe the world around you. This is a perfect moment for what I call "Man With a Poodle" (trademark pending). First person to spot the elusive man with a poodle in the wild wins that day. This can of course be substituted with squirrel holding garbage, lady with a guitar, boy with a ... you get the drift. Quick sidebar: When I first created the game, man with a poodle sightings were extremely rare. Then very quickly they were suddenly everywhere, like a man-poodle invasion of the streets. Ol' Baader-Meinhof at work again!

Even though you must climb on that hamster wheel, whether at home or the office, make sure you take your recess time and literally leave the premise. Go for a walk outside, catch up with a friend over lunch, find a cozy spot and get that next chapter read in the book you cannot put down right now. Do whatever is enjoyable for you and gives you that true mental break. Finish out your day strong with a couple more revolutions on that wheel.

Commuting time (Part Deux)! - see above.

The day is almost over, but you do still have to gets those kiddos to practices and help them with homework. Whether driving yourself, or within a carpool, I always recommend a game of Categories. Not just reserved for long road trips, Categories is a great way to involve everyone and pass the time in traffic in a fun way. Some of my favorites: "Albums/Songs that have a color," "Foods that start with B," or "Whoever's turn it is to carpool gets to pick the category."

When it comes to homework, treat it like school and break it up. If they have 20 minutes to do, at the 10 minute mark take a break and have a pillow fight on the couch. This will reduce both of your levels of stress and frustration for sure.

Dinner Time! Instead of taking this task on solely, make it a group effort. Cooking can be fun when you treat it like a grand experiment in flavor. How could the close to one million Food Network viewers be wrong? Even better, they now have shows featuring kids cooking and baking. So zero guilt over child labor.

You can now see the finish line. A quick clean up, bath time, tuck in, and you're done.

It's late. So forget about watching/reading anything and have sex instead. End your day with a literal bang.

Wash, rinse, and reset for the next day.

Reset instead of repeat in this case because each new day offers up new opportunities to seek out fun. Diversify your portfolio. Try something different. Try not to dwell on the drudgery and wish time away hoping to get to the weekend faster. Don't assume Tuesday is automatically going to be lamer than Saturday. You control the outcome. Live in the now. Be deliberate with your fun. Even if you have a bad day, which of course will happen, know this …

"Every passing minute is another chance to turn it all around" — Cameron Crowe, *Vanilla Sky*

CHAPTER 5

LIVING THE FUN

What if there was an option to do what you want to do instead of what you should do all the time? Can you even imagine how awesome that would be? So many possibilities. Like, *so* so many possibilities. The process of opening your mind to this almost feels like drafting your wish list to Santa. You remember all of the things you ever wanted to do. You get giddy. You know the giddy I mean — the one that hits right before you bubble over with anticipation of what's to come. Ah, is this just a wishful daydream?

Nope. It's not.

Here is the deal: Doing what we want should not just be a wishful hope. We can do what we want, but most times we're just choosing not to. Remember when you were under your parents' rule and all you ever heard was, "When you're an adult you can make your own decisions, until then I am in charge, blah blah blah." Well, last time I checked, we are all adults now, and we do make decisions every day. Some pretty important ones, to boot. The issue is we are not using our decision-making powers wisely for our own benefit. We're constantly focused on what we should be doing and not giving what we want to do a real fighting chance. It's like Superman only flying around for a couple hours on the weekend because Clark's schedule at the Daily Planet is super slammed right now. Boooo! If I could fly, I'd be up there busting barrel rolls through the clouds every day.

It is possible to focus a little more on your wants and still meet everyone else's needs. You can prioritize fun. You are allowed to make that choice as an adult. Bam … empowerment! Heck yeah, feels good. You feel that surge of power rising in you, but then it happens. The faint sound of a swell forming offshore. It slowly builds and builds until it becomes a tidal wave of "Buts" headed for your beach. That big list of all the reasons your situation is so unique and different that this stupid idea of prioritizing fun could never possibly work for you. The wave builds momentum as your list gets longer and longer, until it finally crashes on shore with massive force destroying all hopes of positive action.

Why do we constantly talk ourselves out of fun? Why do we make lame excuses when it comes to trying something different? Why is it weirdly comforting for us to justify to ourselves why we *can't* do things?

Fear plays a big part. My old roommate, Kelly, always loved to sing. In the shower, while cooking up dinner in the kitchen, or just hanging out on the couch, she was always humming something. Because of this I always thought it was so bizarre that every time our group of friends hit up the local karaoke bar, she'd never get on stage and have fun. Of all of us, she loved singing the absolute most. But she always was worried that she wouldn't sound good, or chose a bad song, or mess up. So she'd hang in the crowd and cheer us on instead of getting up there herself and really enjoying the moment.

We're scared of *everything*. Fear of failure. Fear of success. Fear of being judged by others. Fear of looking bad. Fear of appearing less in control, or less successful, or unworthy of respect. Remember, if we're not busy and serious and dialed into that lifestyle at all times, we're not "achieving." Our social worth drops in the eyes of our peers.

So, yeah, fear. So many fears destroying so much fun.

We allow ourselves to believe these false, invalidated feelings as truth and go back to focusing only on the things we need to do — or society expects us to do — and forget about our wants. This self-deception is a real slippery slope back to the meh (and maybe even misery).

The self-deception is poisonous. When we even have a thought of trying something new, we pre-emptively assemble our scapegoat reasons, our list of "buts" and "why nots." We convince ourselves that we don't have enough money, we're too busy, or unprepared, or not talented enough, or will make a fool of ourselves. We rationalize that it's a crazy idea, we're not fit enough, or skinny enough, or attractive enough, or the kicker of kickers, we're too old.

Now, hit pause.

And imagine: What if we put just as much effort into doing something as we did in amassing the list of "buts" in our minds for why we can't/shouldn't/won't?

What if we decided to not overthink it this time and just jump at the chance to try something exciting and fun?

I'm willing to bet a sizable sum that by the time the list of reasons why we couldn't possibly ever climb a mountain is complete, we could actually be setting up our tent at the first base camp on Everest, roasting weenies.

Remember:

"Our doubts are traitors, and make us lose the good we oft might win, by fearing to attempt." —William Shakespeare

Time for Some Serious Debunking

I get it. I strive for as much fun as I can and still know how hard it is to swim through the wave of doubt. *Will I look stupid? Is this a really bad idea?* Even with a perfectly executed duck dive, there's always another wave of hesitation and disbelief waiting to smack you in the face.

The morning I woke up with the idea to write this book, I immediately assembled a huge list of "buts" and "why nots" in my head. Everything from not writing anything of significance since high school, to my lack of expertise with the English language, to the fact that I already had a full-time job and, hence, zero time. It went on and on and on ... sniff, whimper, moan.

But after an exceptional cup of coffee and some perspective, I made the decision. I would put as much effort in to just *doing it* as I would've spent agonizing over should I/shouldn't I for the next couple weeks. I decided to just write it. No backing down. Just barf some words on paper and worry about things like tone, sentence structure, style, and grammar later.

I said fuck it. I dove through the wave and started. And here we find ourselves, you reading, and me somewhere on this great planet with tightly-crossed fingers praying you find some enjoyment and possible nuggets of insight in these pages.

And you know what? *It was fun.*

Everyone has their own individual "buts," of course, but there are some biggies in addition to failure phobia that always seem to lurk on people's excuse lists. So let's take some shots at them, shall we? These seem to be the main offenders I've experienced either personally or through friends over the years.

Lack of money. It is understandable that this is a hang up, as it takes money to buy food, have shelter, and not die. The myth: We think we have to spend a lot of money to create these big, grandiose fun experiences. Don't buy into the marketing, it is just not the case.

For sure, there are cool adventures that require some serious coin, but there are also a ton of free adventures that a lot of us just don't take. I've had the same amount of fun playing a spirited game of Yahtzee on the floor with my son as I've had dropping a Benjamin at Dave & Buster's (no offense, D&B, I love you, too). Creating a DIY sprinkler obstacle course complete with a garbage bag slip n' slide in your backyard can be equally as fun as a pricey trip to the water slide amusement park. Just last summer, our neighbors had a great time planning a stay-cation versus an expensive out of state trip.

To pressure test this, I Googled "can you really have fun if you have no money?" To my surprise, I was instantly presented with a ton of lists of fun ideas that are free.

"103 things to do on a money-free weekend."

"31 things to do when you have no money."

"7 ways to have fun without spending money."

There were some really inventive ideas in these lists that I'd never thought of.

✓ Organize your own self-guided walking tour through town.

✓ Hold a "what's in your cupboard" potluck with your neighbors.

✓ Try your hand at a new skill like origami. Paper pterodactyls anyone?

✓ Assemble and bury a time capsule with your kids.

Now, how dull or wonderful you think these ideas are depends on the mindset you'd bring to them if you did them today. Would you have fun? Or roll your eyes? Either way, find what speaks you. There are definitely great options out there. We just need to flex our collective creative muscles. Adding a little magic to even our mundane tasks increases our fun and doesn't cost anything.

So good news for former paperboy Johnny Gasparini, he will still be able to have fun even if he never gets his two dollars.

Lack of time. The lamest of all. The reality is we have the time, we just waste most of it. We invent meaningless tasks and work to absorb every second, and then complain how busy we are. It goes back to the notion that our society has decided busy means "important." It doesn't.

Even when we do have legitimate work that needs to be completed, we tend to let that work take the available time we have. There's even a name for it: Parkinson's Law, in which work expands to fill space and time. If we have two hours to do a task that in reality only requires one, we'll inevitably take the two hours to git 'er done. Conversely, if we had to complete that same task but were only given one hour, we'd complete it in that one hour without compromising the quality.

These are the crazy mind games we play with ourselves, and I'm guilty, too. I have a detailed sales report that I have to calculate, assemble, and distribute to my team at work each week. This exact same report has taken me, at times, twenty minutes to complete, and at other times an hour. It really depends what day and time I start the report and what's going on around me that dictates its duration. Crazy but true.

So let's stop filling space unnecessarily and take back our time to focus on other, more soul-fulfilling activities. After all, it is all the small decisions we make about how we spend our hours that end up determining how we spend our lives.

Fear of judgment. This is a tough one, because I don't know anyone that hasn't experienced self-consciousness in their lives. It flourishes in adolescence, and if we're lucky, fades for the most part in adulthood. The good news is that nature is on our side with this one. As we get older, we tend to realize what someone should have told us from the very beginning: What other people think about how we look and live our lives just really doesn't matter. Ann Landers famously said, "At age 20, we worry about what others think of us. At age 40, we don't

113

care what they think of us. At age 60, we discover they have not been thinking of us at all."

For those who choose not to believe Ann, fear of judgment can hang around with us, growing uglier as the years pass. Much like an obnoxious zit. From afar it isn't immediately detected, but we know it's there. Similarly we may put on a tough act from afar and appear totally confident, but the second we are challenged to try something new, old Zittie is right there to help dictate all the reasons we won't succeed, and exactly who will be laughing at us. So how do we pop Zittie once and for all?

I think Mark Manson, author of *The Subtle Art of Not Giving a Fuck*, says it best. "There are only so many things we can give a fuck about, so we need to figure out which ones really matter."

I know for fact with every fiber of my being that our own happiness matters WAY more than Barry and Joyce's disapproving side-eye. You see, what others value typically differs greatly from what we value ourselves. It is actually very rare that those values ever line up perfectly. No matter what we do, others may not understand it or approve of it. I suggest we think of these people as the Olympic Russian judge consistently scoring our ice skating routine four points lower than the other judges. Who cares. We expect it, there are other fair judges on the panel (who we might not want to take seriously, either), and we're going to land on the front of the Wheaties box anyway.

So there you have it: Just don't give a fuck.

Try it: "I don't give a fuck."

#IDGAF.

Or, "I'm fresh out of fucks at the moment, so I can't give what I don't have," if you're not into the whole brevity thing.

We need to keep our own opinions and judgments of ourselves in check, too. The problem is, we have a clear picture in our heads of who we are and what our reality is, so much so that we often can't see any other possibilities. The quote, "Whether you say you can or you can't … you're right," has always resonated with me because it speaks so perfectly to the power of the mind and its ability to achieve the unbelievable — or kill a dream instantly.

We really cling to our self-narratives. Like, white-knuckle cling. I cringe every time I hear my fellow mom neighbors say, "I used to be fun." I ask myself, *what does that even mean?* Do they not realize they're the same person they were before? Same brain, same body, all be it slightly older and wiser. I'm pretty sure no one forced them to become dull and sad. They're choosing to allow their current circumstance be the author of their future narrative. They have passed judgment on themselves: *I'm no longer fun or do fun things.* They're being their own Russian judge and don't even realize it.

I think most of us are unaware of the all the judgments we make on ourselves on a daily basis. They can be a bit sneaky and go undetected in some cases. A good rule of thumb is to look for any thought or comment that starts with "I don't". Take a day, or even a week, and really listen to yourself and how you interpret and react to the world around you.

Most people, even those who try hard to be optimists, will find they make a lot of personal judgments and excuses. Expose this bad behavior so you have an opportunity to turn it around. Think of it this way: Why in the world would you project a lame perception of yourself when you could have an awesome one?

Let's shift the conversation in our heads from, "I used to be fun, but now I don't dance anymore," to "I'm fun and dance any chance I get." Sub in any other fun word for dance, too, if that helps (laugh, play, explore, indulge).

Just coming clean and admitting that you make these judgments and excuses is a great first step in shutting them down. Motivational dude Brian Tracy once wrote, "You can make excuses or you can make progress. You choose."

Choose Action

Here's a funny thing about fun. It requires action. We still ultimately have to *do* something. It seems pretty obvious that if you do nothing, nothing will happen. But it's amazing how many of us stumble at the taking action part of things.

The subject of "choosing action" is a common theme in the business world. The idea that taking action, any action, is better than being stuck in a quagmire or not evolving in the face of disruption is prevalent throughout various different industries. Many companies are willing to take the risk of action even though they may lack the knowledge or experience of their competitors in a new venture. Even if unsuccessful, some business leaders believe that missteps or perceived failures resulting from action — as opposed to inaction — ultimately create learnings that will *eventually* lead to success. The fundamental point is that companies have the real potential to succeed at something they may not be particularly good at yet. But they will never have the opportunity to be successful at something without taking action.

Popular business books such as *Failing Forward* by John C. Maxwell, *Ready, Fire, Aim* by Michael Masterson, and the *Do Something* principle by Mark Manson all tout this same theory in unique ways. The message is that the actual doing and learning are far more important and outweigh the risk of potential failure. And I agree. Has there ever been a start-up success story where the company never launched? Never released new products? Never tested new markets?

And yet we've all heard endless success stories in which the initial concept at launch changed as the company took chances, tried new tactics, and pivoted based on experience. Airbnb is a great example of this. What launched as a company renting out air mattresses and breakfast on a shared apartment floor has grown and morphed in a multi-billion dollar home rental business. Sure there were stages during their rise in which they faced shortcomings, new challenges, and had to sell cereal to raise capital, but if they hadn't taken that initial action to try something different we'd all still be staying at overpriced hotels or sketchy hostels.

Apply this action-forward mindset to your pursuit of happiness.

Sound like a stretch, employing business tactics to fun?

Well, let me tell you a story.

A few Christmases ago, my son decided it would be fun to make a gingerbread house. He'd heard about them at school and wanted to do it himself. I of course said yes, then quickly remembered I'd never made one before. Not wanting to dwell on, you know, *details* during this festive time of year, we sprang into action and headed to the store to purchase some graham crackers, icing, and candies. As we launched our gingerbread project with two of his best buddies, it became quickly apparent that we had serious structural issues. If we opened this building to the public, people would die.

We decided on an immediate pivot to build rectangle skyscrapers instead. We then brought in a Lego contractor with limitless bricks so we could build them even higher. We truly scraped the sky. But then we figured, *why stop with just three buildings?* We built more and more, added cool features like zip lines between buildings and even some forts. Now that the city architecture was in place, we decided the finishing touches should include Lego people and Hot Wheels cars and tanks. All adorned in icing and candy of course.

After our new creation was complete, we stepped back and took in its majesty. As our eyes scanned the skyline, it was instantly clear to all of us that it was time to battle.

We waged a four person strike, including a drone air raid on the city. Cracker pieces, Lego bricks, candies, and cars exploded to the delight of us all. In the end, the project was not really gingerbread, and it definitely was not a house, but it was successful in every way imaginable.

Now, what would have happened if we bailed at that first sign of roof trouble?

That's the point. We have to choose action. Create that catalyst. Take the leap, *jump off shit.* Throw caution to the wind and don't overthink it. Don't let your life be the start-up that never launched. That great idea that never came to be.

Launch the fun, and make adjustments as you fly. That is how you bask in the happy.

The Fine Art of Procrastination

In his book, *The Art of Taking Action: Lessons from Japanese Psychology*, author Gregg Krech talks about the peril of inaction. He recognizes that taking action can be stressful, but argues that it can be even more stressful — particularly later on — to procrastinate and leave things untended.

Procrastination is the foundation of inaction. It is basically the gap between intention and action. It's an absurd paradox involving our choice to *avoid* doing something that we know will better ourselves, our situations, our relationships, and our lives. We choose *not* to close that gap, and as a result become more anxious, stressed out, guilt-ridden, and emotionally drained. Pretty abysmal, right?

Who can forget Charlie Kaufman staring at his blank typewriter page while discussing coffee and banana nut muffins with himself....the epitome of procrastination. He is not alone. Joseph Ferrari, a professor of psychology at DePaul University has been a pioneer of research on the subject and has found that 20 percent of all adults are chronic procrastinators. The percentages jump to between 80 and 90 for high school and college students. That definitely explains my many late night test cram sessions. Oh the agony! It's so common that *Psychology Today* named procrastination one of the most common forms of self-sabotage.

I get that action can sometimes be intimidating no matter how much it is hyped. There just may be times where we feel paralyzed to move forward. But because procrastination is a self-inflicted ailment, the good news is that is we can self-correct.

Now, I know I can say we should just choose action over inaction and self-correct until I'm blue in the face, but the fear can rule regardless of what I say. In those times, I think it's best to just embrace the fear. Embrace it, then flip it. Harness its power for good to become unparalyzed. Use it as a motivator and consider: What will happen if you don't take action versus what *could* happen if you do?

Regret Really Sucks. No, Seriously.

"Regret for the things we did can be tempered by time; it is the regret for the things we did not do that is inconsolable." — Sydney J. Harris

We're all familiar with the classic scene of someone near the end of their life. We've seen it played out multiple times in books, TV shows, and movies. Someone old, weak, and propped up with pillows is feeling retrospective. While they are grateful for the good they experienced in their life, they also in that moment become painfully aware of their own regrets.

Of course, the main character sits nearby — the target of this wisdom that will send them into act three with an action plan. So let's say I'm on the deathbed, and you're in the chair next to me.

The dying character (me) rarely ever focuses on the regret of little mistakes or failures that may have happened. Rather, we see me fixate on my regret for the times I didn't take action. The big misses that I can so clearly see now. I regret never asking that person out, or not spending more time with my friends goofing off, or not taking the chance to become the famous rock star I was born to be.

You get the point.

Regret is a negative cognitive and emotional state of loss in which we blame ourselves for a bad or missed outcome. And it sucks.

Regret is powerful my friends. Powerful because we can't change that choice we made. We had one shot at it. It is now firmly stuck in our past, and we're left to just anguish over it. Unfortunately there's no vehicle-agnostic flux capacitor on the market that will allow us to travel back in time to make the corrections we wish we could. Biff is going to stay bully Biff forever in our reality.

It is this missed-opportunity regret that I want us all to avoid. It is for sure the one that freaks me out the most. Honestly, it's one of my greatest fears in life. I don't think anyone should look back on their lives in their golden years and have remorse. We shouldn't have sadness. We should be contently enjoying our last years on earth. Rocking in our chairs, knitting, eating butterscotch hard candies, and playing Uno with our grandkids. We should all feel a sense of accomplishment that although our lives may not have been perfect, we were successful in achieving what really matters: happiness. We prioritized fun and took the action necessary to ensure we had it. We powered through the mid-life meh. We took that chance. We decided to be the kind of person who confidently calls, "Roll the tape!" on their life of awesomeness on their 100th birthday.

So, when presented with a choice tomorrow, choose action and resist living life on the sidelines. Unless you happen to be a pro backup quarterback making $3.2 million to ride the pine, you should be on the field. We all should be on the field. We all should be in the pool. We all should be on the dance floor. We all should be on the plane to someplace cool.

Use the fear of regret to be your motivator toward taking that action now.

"Do or Do Not. There is No Try" –Yoda

Now that you have been scared straight into prioritizing fun, you decide to take action. You actually pull the trigger and go for it. Then something happens. A slight blunder. A roadblock.

Let's say you have a fun recess planned during your work day. It's late August and that special time of year when pumpkin spice is unleashed to the world in the form of our favorite snacks, beverages, and everything everywhere. You know it's cheesy, but there is just something about that fall combo of flavors that tugs at your heart strings. You plan to meet your friend at the park and enjoy your first pumpkin spice latte of the season and catch up. Then Bob From Accounting calls an emergency all-hands on deck lunch meeting to scrub last quarter's financials. Boo Bob! You *suck!* Plan officially blown.

Or let's say one of the activities in your FUN FILE is to take a train ride along the Pacific coast and you've set the plan in motion. You bought the travel book, you selected the week, you convinced a friend to join you. Then out of nowhere the refrigerator craps out. Not only do you have to deal with all of the spoiled food ... you saved the beer and ice cream at least, thank God ... but you now need a new fridge. The funds you were going to use on train tickets evaporate. Plan officially derailed.

These are the times where your arms start to raise up — see them? See them lifting? *You're lifting them* — and the words, "I tried, it didn't work, forget it," form in a dialog bubble next to your head. "Game over" you dramatically exclaim.

Stop. Hit pause. Regroup.

In both these cases the plans were disrupted, not decimated. Just because they couldn't happen as originally planned or imagined doesn't mean they should be completely abandoned. Do you think the Pacific coast will still be there in two months once you have built your funds back up? Do you think maybe you will enjoy that pumpkin spice latte even more with a little bite in the September air and not boiling in a sweater during 78-degree dog days? Of course, a resounding yes to both.

Here is the deal: Little roadblocks will always pop up and people can be too quick to pat themselves on the back and convince themselves they gave it the good ol' college try and stop. Ok, forget that! This logic makes sense if we lived in a perfect world where everything goes 100% to plan and there are never any unexpected deviations. We all know this is not reality. The unexpected will happen. We will go to kick the field goal and the laces won't be out. We will be thrust into Nakatomi Plaza-esque chaotic situations. So what are we going to do? Are we going to Finkle it, and become an Einhorn? Or are we going to shout *"Yippe-ki-yay"* and steal some detonators? It is all about how we react to the disruptions that makes all the difference.

Whenever I ponder the topic of Giving Up, I think of my son during his terrible twos-threes-fours-fives. It's a poignant time because as a new parent you realize you no longer have the luxury of giving up even though it is extremely hard and challenging. You can't say, *oh yeah tried the kid thing, then he blew out his diaper and puked on me, so I quit.*

Additionally for him, as a new being in this world trying to learn how to do basically everything, he of course had frustrating moments. Not everything comes easy, and the desire to want to give up when things aren't going smoothly is strong. I think we can all agree that a pissed off toddler has the propensity to want to rage quit things more often than not.

We were both in unchartered waters, and the next life blowout was inevitable.

It was during this time, I adopted a new mantra: Improvise, Adapt, Overcome. I shouldn't say it's new. Having first heard it from Clint Eastwood in *Heartbreak Ridge*, I loved it for its directness, call to action, and general badass overtone. I knew that it was going to be both my own and Dalton's reactions to the unavoidable blowouts of this period we were experiencing *together* that was going to make the difference between pain and peace. When the shit hit the fan, and the wall, there'd be no giving up. Or whining, for that matter. We would just figure out a new way to continue forward.

My mistakes were plenty. A list so long, profound, and disgusting that decorum prohibits listing them here. Some of the high/lowlights included meal prep (what the hell are they supposed to be eating now?!?), binkie management, car seat manipulation, biting protocol, and rash classification. For Dalton, his blunders centered mainly around his limited possessions. The discovery of the missing stuffed animal at bed time, an inability to follow Lego instructions (and eventually later in life, I'm sure, Ikea instructions), or the struggle to read his new favorite book. In each of these examples we decided together to push through and not give up. I'm happy to report that his stuffed crocodile still resides peacefully in his bed, I now consider myself a semi-professional rash expert, and we are both alive! When you improvise, adapt, and overcome, you just keep doing, and you find new creative ways to reach your goal. And yes, you do reach your goal.

So we all need to ask ourselves: Are we going to be someone who TRIES and gives up, or are we going to be someone that improvises, adapts, overcomes, and continues to DO, regardless of the curveballs? In case the answer isn't obvious, remember the wise words of John Patrick Mason in *The Rock*: "Losers always whine about their best. Winners go home and fuck the prom king/queen."

Beyond just personal resolve and perseverance, I also believe there's a link to quitting tied to complexity. One of the most consistent examples of people trying "their best" and promptly quitting are New Year's resolutions. We all seem to be addicted to making bold proclamations about how we will completely transform the different aspects of our lives come the first of the year. We devise strict and complicated programs, create to-do lists, make major food and exercise overhauls. Even though these attempts are always backed by good intentions, most of us abandon our resolutions. We try, then quit.

In the book *One Word That Will Change Your Life*, authors Jon Gordon, Dan Britton, and Jimmy Page claim that more than two hundred million people (87 percent of U.S. adults) create new goals and resolutions, only to experience the same frustrating results; false starts and failure. According to them, half of all resolution-makers will fail by the end of January. The authors' theory, which I agree with, is that the secret to success is not solely rooted in our strength, but in surrender and simplicity. They suggest selecting one word that will influence your life for a year. By focusing all of your attention on just that one word, and cutting out all of the other noise, you can bring that word to fruition. They claim you don't need complicated plans, just a solid intention toward your one word, and it will manifest in your life.

I believe there is something monumental in simple and direct focus. If something is easily understood by you, and you can execute it naturally, it has more than an amazing chance of being actualized.

Hence the reason I suggest selecting "FUN" as your word for the rest of your life.

CHAPTER 6

SHARING THE FUN

Do you know why Disneyland is referred to as the "Happiest Place on Earth?" Despite some clear gnarly aspects like lines, cost, strollers, and oppressive heat, the majority of the crowd has an underlying excitement to be there. Excited to relive childhood memories. Excited to share new experiences with their own kids. Excited to try that new thrill ride. Excited to not be at work.

Likewise in Las Vegas (Adults-Only Disneyland). Again, despite what appear to be some questionable circumstances like drunkenness, debauchery, and the house always winning, everyone is excited to be there and has an electric anticipation about what might happen. I have done more than my fair share to support the Vegas economy over the years, and I can tell you first-hand there is an *energy* there like nowhere else.

This is no coincidence. It's supported with science. "Emotional contagion" allows one person's emotions and related behaviors to directly trigger similar emotions and behaviors in other people around them. It is the reason why most people are excited when they visit Disneyland and Vegas, and also why, when you're in a bad mood, everyone around you suddenly seems pissed too. Mirror neurons in the brain are the physiological reason behind emotional contagion. They fire when actions are seen and performed by others. Research shows that emotional contagion produces a similar neurological activation or mimicry of one's expressions, vocalizations, postures, and movements with those of another person. The mirror neurons and neural activation act as a functional mechanism to synchronize what is experienced and what is perceived. When people unconsciously mirror their companions' expressions of emotion, they come to feel reflections of those companions' emotions.

So basically, when we're surrounded by people having fun, we cannot help but mimic them and have fun ourselves. We catch the fun through emotional contagion. How awesome is that? Even better, when we're the promoters of fun ourselves, the people in our lives around us feel those positive effects, mimic us, and jump on the fun bandwagon. This is essentially the only time in life where passing something contagious onto others is a good thing. We should all challenge ourselves to be the outbreak monkey of fun for our families and communities. (I can't help but picture that old pyramid shaped infectious disease chart they showed us in middle school. You know the one that started with one stick figure at the top, then terrified us all as it branched out to lower levels of hundreds of people. But this time instead of invoking panic and uneasiness about bubonic plague, it is a magical happy chart of fun contagion adorned with glowing glitter and smiling faces on the hundreds of stick figures at the bottom of the pyramid).

Wouldn't it be cool to live and share our fun every day to infect peers, family members, friends, neighbors, and co-workers? If we can impart a little fun and happiness around us, why wouldn't we? When we seek out the magic in the ordinary, then those that are a part of our daily routines will feel that magic, too. Let's share the exciting adventures we're tackling in our FUN FILE with an invitation to join. We should all work to grow and expand our infectious charts. If we have even just a sliver of the passion and enthusiasm for fun that Buddy the Elf had for Christmas, I am confident our own little worlds will start to change for the better, one stick figure at a time.

Club Membership

Most of us have been a part of some type of club in our lives. It could have been a secret society, a hobby group, an institution, a social movement, or even just a shared love for something. Whatever the club, once we became a part of it, we bonded with other members from that shared experience. We became forever in-the-know together, connected by participation, and in on the jokes. That bond stays secure no matter how much time passes. And when we cross paths and encounter other members in the wild, we give each other that knowing look of acknowledgement, a special gesture, or a shout-out.

There have been two times in my life when I became part of a club and felt that bond of inclusion.

For completely random and genius reasons, I decided to attend Washington State University. Once I set foot on that campus, I magically became a Cougar forever. There's something special about that time in your life when you're surrounded by people all the same age, all doing the same thing, and all figuring it out together. It wasn't until I graduated and moved to California that I felt the real impact of what that meant. I thought that once I left the campus and that little bubble of existence my association of being a Coug would be a closed chapter. That's why I'll never forget the first time I was at the San Diego airport and heard someone shout "Go Cougs!" I was wearing a WSU hat so I popped up like a meerkat and swiveled around to find the perpetrator. A stranger walking by with a smile gave me the nod, and I returned a hearty "Go Cougs" back. I didn't know him, but we instantly felt that connection. We were part of the same tribe. Although rare, I do have other Cougar sighting, sometimes when I least expect it. I've been at the dentist, shopping for furniture, meeting a new business partner, and visiting the

Acropolis in Athens, Greece (true story). No matter the locale, every time I spot one, I get the same interaction, the same shout-out. It always makes me feel nostalgic and special.

Another time: Last year on a six-hour drive home from a spring ski trip in Mammoth Mountain, our tired sedan — practically on life support already — lost its ability to produce conditioned air. Not normally that big a deal, when driving through the desert with two sweaty and complaining little boys in the backseat, the ante was upped. As we pulled in the driveway successfully completing the ride from hell, our spirits quickly lifted as we realized this meant we were in the market for a new car. I'd never really been "into cars," mostly because I could never afford anything extravagant, and I was just focused getting from point A to B.

This time, however, my husband and I decided to get something more fun. Something that would perfectly accent our awesomeness. So we got a cherry-red Jeep Wrangler. Our goal was to feel like we were on vacation in Hawaii every time we left the house. And our new baby really delivered. With the sun on my shoulders, the wind whipping through my hair, and the music blaring, I rolled down the streets of my neighborhood like I'm on my way to Waikiki beach. I now actually look forward to running humdrum errands. After about a week or so of tooling around in it, I started to notice other Jeep owners (Baader-Meinhoff strikes again). Every time they'd pass me on the street, or we were both stopped at a light, I'd get this nod with a "we know how fun Jeeps are" wave. It was totally unexpected, but I have to admit that every time I get one, it makes me feel happy and unique. I feel a connection with that stranger.

The power of these types of bonds comes from the exclusivity, not everyone is a part of it. It's just cool to be involved in something a little exclusive. It makes us feel special when we spot a member or they spot us. We acknowledge each other and enjoy the camaraderie. It's like that feeling you get when you meet a new group of people for the first time, and someone busts out your favorite quote from an obscure movie. Even though you have never met that person, and you may have nothing else in common with them, you can't help but feel connected by that. You know deep down that they have to be at least a little badass given their superb taste in cinema.

I think about prioritizing fun in the same way. Once it becomes part of your life, you're in the club. A secret, exclusive club of awesome people putting fun first, enjoying life, and walking around happy. It's like the Illuminati, but without the creepy old dudes.

Get Yourself a Sponsor

A couple years ago in October, I randomly decided to create a haunted house. Halloween is my favorite holiday, so it was not completely out of left field, but the idea just seemed to pop into my head. It was, of course, met with extreme enthusiasm from my son Dalton. We were going to create a scare house in my driveway and backyard for the whole neighborhood to visit. I'd never attempted anything like this before, nor had I been to many homemade houses, but my excitement ticket was already punched and I had a vision, so we boarded the train and decided to worry about the details as they came. Clearly, a common theme for me.

On opening weekend, myself, my husband, and eight little boys got to work setting it up. We were successful on both the creepy and gory fronts, and quite happy with the outcome. It looked legit. Everyone that went through both screamed and raved about the great time they had. One of the best parts of the haunted house was my good friend Shannon acting as the ghoulish tour guide. He summoned his inner actor, was in full character, and brought all of the scenes to life. He totally stole the show. That night both Shannon and I had some next level fun scaring children and creating lasting memories. We just enjoyed it in different ways. For Shannon, the work of building and tearing down a complete haunted house seemed overwhelming and daunting … basically the opposite of fun for him. For me, although it was entertaining to terrorize the people as they walked through, the aspect of coming up with the ideas and creating them together with my son and friends was what was most fun for me. In this particular case, Shannon leaned on me to enjoy an experience he probably wouldn't have come up with himself.

We are familiar with the concept of sponsors as they relate to addiction recovery and accountability: A person you can depend on to be that constant positive force in your life, keeping you on track. I have always thought a sponsor would be a welcomed addition to anyone's life, even if they're not struggling with a serious issue. I know I can always use a positive voice of reason and supportive reminders. I also like the idea of leaning on someone else from time to time. So when it comes to fun, I say set yourself up for success and get a sponsor.

That Halloween, I was Shannon's sponsor for fun. Sponsors help create opportunities you would otherwise not participate in. Ideally, you both have a sponsor and act as a sponsor for someone else. This give-and-take only maximizes your opportunities. I'd vaguely heard of the game Bunco (known in some circles as Drunko), but I never had a real interest to learn or play it. If it wasn't for my friend Amy's call asking me to play as a substitute in her group, I'd still be a Bunco virgin to this day. So instead of my normal weeknight routine, I decided to go ahead and join them. It's a silly game for sure, but I ended up having a ton of fun laughing and getting to know new people. Definitely more fun than I would have just staying home. Amy was my sponsor for fun that night.

The other key benefit to having a sponsor is that they can act as our lifeguards for fun. They stand watch in their towers as we swim out navigating the deep end of life, and rescue us if we start to drown in negativity (they don't have to necessarily look good running in slow-motion down a beach, but it's nothing to discourage, either). It's tough to stay in tune with our fun-jo and prioritize fun when we feel anxious and stressed out. And we will given the world we live in today.

The news cycle is a big culprit and makes it near impossible to escape. A 2018 survey by the American Psychological Association showed that one in ten adults check the news *every hour*. Additionally a full 20 percent report they constantly monitor their social media feeds, which expose them to the latest headlines whether they want to see them or not. In this survey, more than half of Americans claim the news causes significant stress, sadness, problems sleeping, mood swings, and even aggressive behavior.

It's not just about trying to stay informed these days, it is about trying to stay informed while maintaining your mental health. It's not crazy that we feel like we survive the news rather than consume it. Over the last fifteen to twenty years the way in which our news is presented has significantly changed. Graham Davey, a professor emeritus of psychology at Sussex University in the UK and editor-in-chief of the *Journal of Experimental Psychopathology*, says today's news is "increasingly visual and shocking," and points to the inclusion of smartphone videos and audio clips as examples. Some of Davey's research has shown that negative TV news is a significant mood-killer and that this change in mood exacerbates the viewer's own personal worries, even when those worries are not even directly relevant to the news stories being broadcast.

So if we know that the news can be a slippery mental slope from upbeat to beat down, why do we keep going back for more? I think it is very akin to rubber necking at a crash on the freeway. We all rant and yell at the traffic ahead of us knowing that it is unnecessary because the road itself is not technically blocked. Yet when it is our turn to pass by the crash, we slow down and gape at it ourselves.

We're not purposeful hypocrites. Nature is working against us on this one with a concept called "negativity bias." It means the human brain is wired to pay attention to instances and information that scares or unsettles us. Our instinctual survival depends on both seeking out rewards and avoiding harm, but it's the avoiding harm bit that always takes precedence. Makes sense that our caveman brothers and sisters concentrated more on saber-tooth tiger attacks than arranging the animal skins for a cozy night of "cave drawings and chill."

So how can we maintain our fun-jo and positivity in light of all this?

Simply recognizing that this negativity bias risk exists is a good first step toward not becoming overwhelmed by it. This knowledge helps us identify when we're dwelling on the negative aspects of a situation, or worse, drowning in it. We can experience our natural moment of alarm, and then take a more proactive attempt in letting it go. And if you feel you need a little help getting back to your happy, then that is where your sponsor comes in. Just signal to them to toss you the life preserver and drag you back from the depths.

I recall a story about Steven Spielberg. When he was deep into filming *Schindler's List* and in a very dark place each day, Robin Williams called him at night to get him laughing again. Yup, Robin Williams was Spielberg's fun sponsor on *Schindler's List*. It's amazing how having just a quick little conversation with a sponsor can be all you need to get yourself back on track and in a cheerful space.

My husband Rob happens to be a world-class fun sponsor. He always has an uncanny way of being upbeat and excited about something right in those moments where my negativity bias is all-consuming. If I had a crummy day at the office and barge in the front door with a scowl on my face, he'll be the one that exclaims, "Look at the sweet 1000-piece Star Wars puzzle Amazon just delivered, and I found a new bourbon cocktail recipe for us to try!" Scowl successfully erased. Since it is humanly impossible for anyone to be super-happy every second of the day, he's a great balancer for me.

I encourage everyone to seek out fun sponsors around them ... just not Rob. He is unfortunately not accepting any new applicants at this time because I am hoarding him for myself. And while friends and family do make stellar sponsors, I think we should also be open to find them in unlikely places. That co-worker you don't really know, or the dude that jogs on the treadmill next to you every night at the gym could be phenomenal sponsors if we gave them a chance. They could become that little bright light you look forward to joking with every day.

Also don't be too quick to overlook or dismiss potential "situational" sponsors. These are the people that pop into your life I learned this first-hand when I was the head of sales at a start-up company and spent the majority of my time on the road by myself. Trust me that there would've been many a cross country flight that would've majorly sucked had I not opened up to the fun sponsor seated next to me in 15B.

Strangers are not *always* weirdos. Most are interesting people who have more in common with us than we realize. So reach out. You never know who may be prioritizing fun as well.

Avoid the Saboteurs

While amassing a solid stable of fun sponsors is great, you must also beware of fun saboteurs. You know who they are. The vampires in the room sucking the joy and amusement out of everything. They sit there tapping their long grinchy finger against their chin judging, scoffing, and spewing negativity while all of us Whos are just trying to enjoy our impromptu game of charades. They can't or won't participate in the fun themselves (often because of their own personal issues) and therefore don't want anyone else to enjoy it either. These killjoy's actions can be deliberate, or unwitting, but the result is always the same. Lameness.

As you flex your fun-jo muscle more and more, two things will happen. Fellow fun prioritizers will start to unexpectedly appear. They will join in on the fun as supporters and possibly become sponsors. At the same time the fun saboteurs will come out of the woodwork as well. They will be off put by your general joyful demeanor and carefree attitude, and mobilize their campaigns of destruction. Just as Pat Healy painted a pitiful picture of *Roller Pig*, these guys do not have your best interest at heart. They have their own agendas, and problems they are projecting on you. Witnessing happiness, when they are unable to attain it themselves, makes them uncomfortable, jealous, and bent on disruption.

Sabotage is a common theme in the world of health and fitness. There are close to thirty magazines in the United States alone dedicated to the subject. There are countless websites, blogs, and social groups. All of these provide practical advice on avoiding diet and exercise saboteurs. Granted many of the examples involve a coworker deliberately leaving donuts outside your cubical, or a friend repeatedly flaking on your yoga class, but the overall message on how handle these situations I think is applicable.

Taking cues from the industry, the best solution I have employed in my life is; *Do Not Engage*. Simply block them out. Ignore them. Reject their negativity. Refuse to participate in their scheme.

My favorite fortune cookie quote that I have never forgotten is "you give power to what you give attention to". Given my love of Chinese food and all things dumpling-related, there have been a lot of fortunes read. This one really sticks with me because it is so powerful and true. When you engage with saboteurs you are giving them power. You are letting them into your world and allowing them to have a level of influence over you. By simply not engaging, you revoke your attention from them, and they are powerless to affect your fun.

A good tool to help you avoid engagement with these downers? Your good ol'Predator mask. Just as it highlights all potential opportunities for fun around you, it likewise blocks out what is not. The saboteurs and the naysayers will be greyed out in your field of vision. They will no longer exist and you can fixate on your fun.

Prioritize Fun: The Movement

As I mentioned, all of this happened when I started to take careful notice of the people around me. I noticed that my over-busy peers, who had many of the traditional measures of success on lock, appeared exhausted and not overly joyful. I questioned what the ultimate goal really was for life and what success truly looked like. I also questioned why I seemed to be having a different experience in my life when I shared so many common traits with my peers. I had the same challenges, the same frustrations, the same family drama, and quite frankly even more personal failures than most in my friend group. I also felt the sting of getting older, had unrelenting work stress, and felt the pressure of parenthood and the desire to raise a likeable human.

But with all that, I was somehow just a little bit more playful, a little more excited about each day, and generally always in a happy mood. That led me to develop my theory about fun, the need to have more of it, and the need to prioritize it. You see, having more fun was the *only* real difference when I measured myself against my peers. I'd always led with fun. That was consistently top of mind for me no matter what the project, experience, or task was. The question I'd always ask myself was, "Okay, so this is what needs to happen, how can I make this fun for me?"

Some will say that perspective is a little selfish, but I contend that I just have my priorities straight (wink-wink). As I explored this theory, did more research, and tested it out on my unsuspecting friends, I became overwhelmingly convinced of the simplicity and power of prioritizing fun. This basic notion of fun really did have the ability to make people happier. Connecting these dots in my brain made me want to share the concept with the world. I want people to lean into fun with extreme prejudice and experience more joy in their lives every day.

And then a funny thing happened as I wrote this book. When I get excited about something, I'm a notorious over-sharer. I can't help myself. I would talk about prioritizing fun with everyone I knew. It was nice to get other people's feedback and initial thoughts on things, but I wasn't expecting anything else. But gradually the conversation shifted from me talking about it/asking them questions to my friends bringing it up to me.

It seemed that prioritizing fun was more than just an interesting idea or anecdote you hear one day then quickly forget the next. My friends really seemed to embrace the belief and take it to heart. They willingly, without prompting from me, challenged themselves to make small fun-forward changes in their own lives.

I was suddenly regaled with their latest adventures. My co-workers bragged to me more about their fun breaks than their workload. When passing my neighbors on the street, they'd give me the wink and promise me that they had made time for fun that day. With all of these interactions, I saw people really being more exuberant in their routines. I saw them organically forming a special club, and I saw them in turn infecting their friends and family with fun as well. Maybe it is because fun itself is so inviting, or maybe it is that fact that trying something new always brings people together, but fun quickly became a movement in my little area of this world.

I was inspired by this to create a community around prioritizing fun because to me it is very simple: Life and fun are better when shared.

I encourage you to join the movement @prioritizefun and share your stories, journey, and photographic evidence of fantastic fun. Get inspired, laugh, and steal the amazing ideas you may not have ever thought of yourself.

Every movement needs a symbol, of course. I thought it would be cool to have an unspoken way to identify other members. *Fight Club* had black eyes and bandaged noses, but I figure something like a hand gesture is more appropriate. The peace sign of fun, if you will. Fun can take many unique forms, but the one common thread is that it is always rooted in our hearts. It therefore made sense to me to form an "F" — for fun — with your right hand and place it over your heart. It is and instant identifier of the mission, and admittedly a little addicting once you start.

With a little help from a designer friend, we transformed this hand gesture into an official Prioritize Fun logo. I think of it as a badge of honor for happiness.

I wanted to share a few snapshots of my peer group that are now part of the movement and eagerly flash their tribe gesture whenever possible. I challenge you to do the same and see how a community begins to grow around you as well.

So, In Closing Arguments ...

I realize within this book I have vilified over-complicated regimens and super long to-do lists to a degree, BUT even I cannot deny the appeal of a concise Top 10 takeaway list to tie all of this rambling together. So here it is. Of course my Top 10 list goes to 11 ... just like my amps.

1. A measure of your busyness is not a measure of your value.
2. Recognize that happiness is what really matters.
3. Know that fun is the one guaranteed method to achieve happiness.
4. Commit to prioritizing fun in your everyday life and tap into your fun-jo.
5. Create and execute your FUN FILE and find the magic in the ordinary.
6. Choose to take action and live your fun.
7. Overcome your wave of "buts" and "why nots" and resist the temptation to quit.
8. Share your fun with the people in your life.
9. Partner with a fun sponsor (or ten!).
10. Join the movement and become part of the #prioritizefun community.
11. Always go for it on fourth down....fortune favors the bold.

A special thanks to all of the awesome people in my life that put up with my craziness, encourage my endeavors, and join me on my adventures. I am grateful to know you all, and inspired by the new people I meet every day on this crusade of fun. A special shout out to my core posse Rob and Dalton who are the definition of badass.

I Would Really Love to Hear From You …

and I'm not just saying that!

Did Prioritize Fun make an impression on you? Got something to share? An idea, new perspective, or personal anecdote? I am always eager for feedback and encourage you to write a review, or contact me directly at

nanci.prioritizefun@gmail.com

Like Clark Griswold, I'm on a quest. A quest for fun. It's my personal mission to continue to push myself to explore new things, and share those experiences on my blog. You can keep up with my motivational musings at

www.prioritizefun.com

Made in the USA
Middletown, DE
30 November 2020